MARX
LIFE AND WORKS

Facts On File Chronology Series

MARX
LIFE AND WORKS

Maximilien Rubel

Translated by Mary Bottomore

Facts On File, Inc.
119 West 57 Street, New York, N.Y. 10019

First published in 1980 by

Facts On File, Inc.
119 West 57 Street
New York, N.Y. 10019

ISBN 0-87196-516-X

Typeset by Leaper and Gard Ltd, Bristol

Printed in Great Britain

Contents

General Introduction to the Chronology Series

The aim of this series is to provide an accurate, succinct, in-depth account of the central figure's life and ideas and the impact he had on the events of his day. Personal details are included when they shed light on character and personality. The subject's own writings and speeches are the main source of information, but letters and the opinions of his contemporaries are used when they add a useful extra dimension to the study. An attempt has been made only to record verifiable facts and to provide a reliable, up-to-date account of the subject's activities and influence. The main events of the time are included so as to set the person in historical perspective and to provide a rational context for his ideas and actions. Bibliographical references are given so as to permit readers, should they so desire, to follow up the quotations; a detailed bibliography of works by and about the subject is also included.

Martin McCauley, Series Editor

Preface to the English Edition

This English translation is a somewhat expanded version of the *Chronologie* presented in the first volume of the Pléiade edition of Marx's 'Economy' (Paris: Gallimard, 1963, 5th ed. 1977, p. LVII–CLXXVI).

Within its more limited scope this *Marx Chronology* has the same purpose as the author's previous publications in this field; namely, to provide the non-specialised reader with sufficient biographical and factual data to enable him to become acquainted with the personality and work of Karl Marx, rescued from travesties and parodies, and liberated from the received ideas about the teachings of a thinker and political militant who once modestly described his activity in the following terms: 'I am a machine condemned to devour books and to throw them in a changed form on the dunghill of history.'

The definitive biography of Marx has yet to be written. It should provide an unbiased portrait of the man and the thinker whose work, if disentangled from the legendary, mythical and ideological encumbrances which hinder access to it, will be seen as an attempt, sustained under the most unfavourable material and moral circumstances, to contribute to the emancipation of humanity through the conscious activity of 'the immense majority in the interest of the immense majority.' (*Communist Manifesto*)

When Marx, shortly before his death, declared that he was not a 'Marxist', it was not in order to condemn one category of disciples and to show his preference for another, but to indicate his support of a fundamental principle: the cause of the labour movement ought not to be linked to the name of any thinker, however great his creative genius. Tolerating the use by his followers of the terms 'Marxist' and 'Marxism' meant betraying the spirit of a theory, the originality of which was precisely that it had been conceived as the expression of the will and consciousness of a social class, 'the most numerous and the poorest class' (Saint-Simon). That would have been a concession to vanity, and involved the risk of having his name associated with the activities of a political sect and the aberrations of a moral ideology. (Cf. M Rubel, *Marx, critique du marxisme*, Paris: Payot, 1974, p. 403)

The preceding passage embodies my justification of the field of research which I call 'Marxology'. I conceive it as an intellectual reaction of 'self-defence' against the spread of the obscurantist ideologies which, by invoking an alleged system of thought called 'Marxism', make use of of Marx's social theory for purposes of political oppression and economic enslavement. A meticulous search through the thousands of pages written by Marx would never discover a single line to justify an assertion such as the following:

'dialectical and historical materialism was the most important discovery in human thought, a veritable revolution in science, philosophy and universal knowledge.' (MEW, Vol. I, 1966, preface, p. IX)

Nor would it provide the slightest support for the statement:

'The dialectical materialist philosophy elaborated in creative collaboration by Marx and Engels, together with their political economy and scientific communism, are an intrinsically complete system of philosophical, economic and socio-political doctrines: they represent the only scientific Weltanschauung.' (Introduction to the new Marx-Engels-Gesamtausgabe, I, 1, Moscow–Berlin, 1975, p. 20)

It is unnecessary, I think, to refer to the incisive criticism made by Karl Popper in order to condemn such verbal excesses, which betray the state of mind, characterised by a lust for domination, of a new class of masters. Marx's work embodies theoretical principles and ethical arguments which dispose of the pseudo-science called 'historical materialism', with all its attendant 'historicist' myths and epistemological aberrations.

By way of conclusion let me cite a passage from a text which may be regarded as the theoretical complement of the present *Chronology*:

'In the *Communist Manifesto* Marx speaks of the "theoretical conclusions of the Communists", which "merely express, in general terms, actual relations springing from an existing class struggle, from a historical movement going on under our very eyes." These are conclusions derived from the empirical study of historical and social facts, but not a new "scientific socialism". At the most they constitute a science *of* socialism, an analysis of an existing socialist movement and of the conditions in which it develops.' (T B Bottomore and M Rubel, Introduction to *Karl Marx: Selected Writings in Sociology and Social Philosophy* London: Watts & Co., 1956, p. 16)

M.R.
Paris, December 1979

The titles in italics under each year or period of years indicate Marx's principal writings during that time. The letter P after a title indicates a posthumously published work; it is followed by the date of first publication.

The principal sources used are: the works and correspondence of Marx and Engels in various collected editions; the Marx-Engels archives of the International Institute of Social History in Amsterdam; for those texts which are missing from the collected editions: Karl Marx, *Chronik seines Lebens in Einzeldaten*, Moscow 1934; O Mänchen-Helfen and B Nicolaïevski, *Karl und Jenny Marx*, Berlin 1933; the work of Heinz Monz, *Karl Marx, Grundlagen der Entwicklung zu Leben und Werk*, Trier 1973.

1818–1835

May 5 1818: Born in Trier (Prussian Rhineland), the second son among eight children of Heinrich Marx (1782–1838), a lawyer, and Henriette, née Pressburg (1787–1863), both descended from rabbinical families. Two brothers and two sisters of Karl will die of tuberculosis in their youth. To escape from the situation of the Jews after the fall of Napoleon and the union of the Rhineland with Prussia, Karl's father, a moderate liberal, patriot and follower of Voltaire, was converted to protestantism between 1817 and 1819.

1824: The Marx children are baptised as protestants.

1825: Karl's mother also baptised. Protestantism was the religion of a minority of the Catholic Rhineland.

1830: Karl enters the Friedrich-Wilhelm Gymnasium in Trier.

1835–1841

Reflections of a Young Man on the Choice of a Profession (P, 1929)
Wild Songs (1841)
The Philosophy of Nature in Democritus and Epicurus (1841) (P)

1835 (August–September): Karl passes his school leaving examinations. He writes in his German composition (*Reflections of a Young Man on the Choice of a Profession*) '. . . To some extent, our relations with society have begun to be established before we are able to determine them . . . the main idea which should guide us in choosing a profession is the good of humanity and our own perfection . . . Man's nature is such that he can attain his own perfection by working for the welfare and perfection of his fellows.'

1835 (October): Marx begins to study law at the University of Bonn. He also takes courses in classical mythology and the history of art. During his time in Bonn (until March 1836) he joins actively in student life and is a member of a group of poets.

1836 (August): Marx obtains the University of Bonn leaving certificate. During the summer holidays in Trier he becomes secretly engaged to his childhood playmate, Jenny, four yours his senior (1814–1881), the daughter of Ludwig von Westphalen (1770–1842), a Prussian state councillor, and of Karoline, née von Heubel. Jenny is a descendant of members of the Scottish aristocracy, the Campbells of Argyle. One of her ancestors, Archibald, Earl of Argyle, was beheaded in Edinburgh for rebelling against James II. Jenny's step-brother, Ferdinand von West-phalen (1799–1876) will later become Prussian Minister of the Interior. Jenny's brother, Edgar, a classmate of Marx, will join the young couple in their political struggles in Brussels in 1846.

1836 (October): Marx enrolls in the Faculty of Law of the University of Berlin, and studies the Pandects with F K Savigny, criminal law with E Gans (a Hegelian and admirer of Saint-Simon), and anthropology with H Steffens. He sends Jenny three notebooks of lyrical poems and epigrams, many of which he offered to his father on his birthday.

Conflict between Karl and his father because of the secret engagement. The father loves and greatly admires his son, but knows and fears the 'demoniac' and 'Faustian' nature which may draw him into an equivocal situation with regard to Jenny's family, and compromise her reputation. 'There is no more sacred duty for a man than the one he assumes towards the weaker woman . . .' (letter to his son, November 9).

1837: Marx continues his studies in law, but also attends courses in philosophy and history. At the *Doktorklub*, a group of Hegelian writers and academics, he becomes friendly with the Bauer brothers, Bruno and Edgar, Karl Friedrich Köppen and others. He writes poetry and tries his hand at novels and plays. In a candid letter to his father (November 10 1837) he describes his tormented life and his studies in Berlin. Law, poetry, philosophy; an attempt at a 'new metaphysical system'; sleepless nights, solitude, illness. 'A curtain had fallen, my sanctuary had been desecrated and new gods had to be put there. Starting out from idealism, which I had compared to and nourished with that of Kant and Fichte, I decided to seek the Idea in the real itself.' He had read fragments of Hegel whose 'harsh, grotesque melody' had displeased him; he had attempted a philosophic-dialectical analysis of the concept of divinity in its religious, natural and historical manifestations. 'My last sentence was the beginning of the Hegelian system; this task for which I had familiarised myself to some extent with natural science, Schelling, and history, and which (for it was meant to be a new logic) is written in such a confused style that I myself can hardly make it out now — this darling child of mine, nurtured in moonlight, carries me like a treacherous siren into the hands of the enemy.' The enemy is Hegel, whom the ailing Marx studies 'from beginning to end; and the majority of his disciples too.' In his letter Marx also speaks of the habit he has acquired of making excerpts from the books he is reading and scribbling down his reflections on them.

1838 (May 10): Death of his father, whose last letter expresses dissatisfaction and sadness concerning his son's moral crisis, but also shows faith in his vocation. In Berlin, Marx is declared unfit for military service, owing to a weak chest and the coughing up of blood, both in 1838 and 1839.

1839: Marx works all year on his doctoral thesis (on the Epicurean, Stoic and Sceptical philosophies) with the idea of obtaining a teaching post in Bonn, following the example of his friend, Bruno Bauer. The latter pesters and encourages him to get the examination over quickly. This is only a 'farce' for everything has still to be done in Prussia where, in the absence of political interests, universal interests are richer and more complex than anywhere else. Reading of Aristotle, with a view to a critique of Trendelenburg's *Logical Investigations*.

1840: While working on his thesis, Marx plans to write polemical, indeed satirical, essays against the attempts to reconcile religion and philosophy in certain university circles (G Hermes, K P Fischer). Karl F Köppen publishes a pamphlet, *Frederick the Great and his Adversaries*, which is a defence of the philosopher king and a profession of faith in favour of reason and progress; it is dedicated 'to my friend Karl Heinrich Marx, of Trier.' For Köppen, the greatness of Frederick II lies in his having united Epicureanism, Stoicism and Scepticism in his thought. In a letter to her son (May 29, 1840) Marx's mother complains of the unfriendly attitude of the Westphalen family toward her since the death of his father.

1841: Philosophical readings (Spinoza, Leibniz, Hume, Kant, etc.).

3

January 23: *Wild Songs*, Marx's first publication, appears in *Athenäum*, a review founded by members of the 'Doctors' Club'. Marx writes his doctoral thesis which later, when preparing it for publication, he will dedicate to his future father-in-law, his 'dear, paternal friend', L von Westphalen, a follower of Saint-Simon, who had made him understand that 'idealism is not a chimera, but a truth'. Against the determinism of Democritus, Marx espouses the Epicurean principle of the freedom of consciousness and man's capacity to influence nature. In the preparatory notes for his thesis he defends the Epicurean ethic against the conventional moralism of Plutarch. From all this work there emerges an intention to criticise and to fight, a will to realise the philosophy of consciousness in its conflict with a world borne along by two currents: the first, that of liberalism which has philosophy as its principle and criticism as its activity; the second, positive philosophy, which remains closed in upon itself, never going beyond demands and tendentiousness. 'It is not ideology (!) nor vaingloriousness which we need for our life, but to live without confusion.' Marx receives his doctorate from the Faculty of Philosophy of the University of Jena (April 15). In a letter (September 2) to the novelist Berthold Auerbach, Moses Hess, (the author of *The Sacred History of Mankind* (1837), in which he preaches a messianic communism and *The European Triarchy* (1841) in which he sets out a philosophy of action leading to the social and economic emancipation of mankind) calls Marx 'the greatest, perhaps the one genuine philosopher now alive'; in spite of his youth 'he will give mediaeval religion and politics their *coup de grâce*;' he combines in his person Rousseau, Voltaire, Holbach, Lessing, Heine and Hegel. Marx travels to Bonn and becomes closely connected with Bruno Bauer; he expects to publish with him and L Feuerbach a review called *Atheist Archives*, more radical than the *German Annals* of A Ruge, one of the representatives of the Hegelian Left. As a result of proposing a Left Hegelian toast at a banquet in honour of the Liberal deputy Welcker, Bruno Bauer is suspended from his post at the University of Bonn (October). A month later he publishes anonymously *The Trumpet of the Last Judgment on Hegel, the Atheist and AntiChrist. Ultimatum*. Some parts of this pamphlet which, under the pretext of denouncing Hegel's atheism, presents the philosophy of universal consciousness in opposition to Hegel's World Spirit, were possibly written by Marx.

1842

The Proceedings of the Sixth Rhenish Diet
Leading article in No 179 of the "Kölnische Zeitung"
The Philosophical Manifesto of the Historical School of Law
Communism and the Augsburg "Allgemeine Zeitung"
Supplement to nos 335 and 336 of the Augsburg "Allgemeine Zeitung"
on the assemblies of estates in Prussia.

January–February: Marx returns to Trier where he remains until the death of Ludwig von Westphalen (March 3).

February: Marx sends Ruge *Remarks on the latest Prussian Instruction on the Censorship.* Intended for the *German Annals*, Marx's article, signed 'a Rhinelander', will appear a year later in *Anekdota*, a review also directed by Ruge, and published in Zurich: here Ruge publishes articles whose publication in Dresden is forbidden by the Prussian censorship. The article ends with this quotation from Tacitus: 'How rare and fortunate are those times when one can think as one wishes and say what one thinks.'

March 5: Marx tells Ruge he will soon be sending him two essays; in the first he discusses Christian art and in the second criticises Hegel's philosophy of law. 'Essentially, it is an attack on constitutional monarchy, a completely misbegotten contradictory creature which destroys itself. *Res publica* has no equivalent in German'. Marx writes to Ruge (March 20) that he has expanded the essay on Chrisian art into a study of 'religion and art considered in relation to Christian art', but that the work needs to be completely recast. A few days later he says that he is nearly ready and promises to send Ruge four essays: '1. *On religious art*, 2. *On the Romantics*, 3. *The philosophical manifesto of the Historical School of Law*, 4. *The positive philosophers.*' The study notebooks that are known from this period relate to the following subjects: C Meiner (General critical history of religions, 1806-1807), Jean Barbeyrac (Treatise on the ethics of the Church Fathers, 1728), De Brosse (On the cult of fetish-gods . . . 1785), C A Böttiger (Ideas on the Mythology of Art, 1826-1836), J J Grund (Greek painting . . . 1810-1811), C F von Rumohr (Italian explorations). Only the third of the essays mentioned was published.

April: Marx settles in Bonn and begins his collaboration with the

Rheinische Zeitung (founded on January 1, 1842) with a series of essays on the debates of the 6th Rhenish Diet, which had sat in Düsseldorf from May to July 1841. The first essay (on the freedom of the press) will appear in May in six numbers of the paper; the censor bans the second essay (on the ecclesiastical conflict in Cologne); the third (on the law against the gathering of fire-wood) will appear in five parts in October and November. On this last essay and on the articles he will publish in 1843 (on the poverty of the Moselle winegrowers), Marx will observe in 1859 that they provided him for the first time with the opportunity to turn his attention to economic questions. He will also say that at that time he had only mistrust for the pale 'philosophical echoes' of French socialism and communism in the columns of the *Rheinische Zeitung* while recognising his incompetence to discuss them. In fact, it was through the articles of Moses Hess and G Mevissen, published in the same paper, that Marx became familiar with Saint-Simonian and socialist and communist ideas, but without giving great importance to them at that time.

May–July: Marx visits Trier on the death of his brother. He is refused the material help he had expected from his family. 'It is truly fortunate that public infamy prevents a man of character from allowing himself to be irritated by private injustice.' (Marx to Ruge, July 7)

October 15: Installed in Cologne, Marx takes over as managing editor of the *Rheinische Zeitung*. He writes a reply to an attack in the Augsburg *Allgemeine Zeitung* which accused *RhZ* of communist tendencies. In this article Marx mentions for the first time the names of Fourier, Leroux, Considerant, and speaks of the 'penetrating works' of Proudhon. He announces that the *RhZ* will submit their ideas to a 'thorough critical examination.'

November: Irritated by the articles in the *RhZ* on the distress of the Moselle winegrowers, von Schapper, the first president of the Rhine province, launches official denials and accuses the *RhZ* of false reporting, calumny and incitement to disaffection. Friedrich Engels, en route to England, visits the editor of the *RhZ*. The meeting with Marx lacks warmth, as the latter believes Engels to be close to the 'Free', a group of Berlin Liberals, correspondents of the *RhZ* with whom Marx will publicly break off relations.

December: In several articles Marx criticises the corporative constitution of the Prussian state and compares the fiscal situation of landowners in France, England and Prussia. 'Because of their peculiar composition, the Diets are nothing more than an association of special interest, which are privileged to assert their particular concerns against the state. Consequently, they are legally constituted bodies of non-state elements within the state . . . the particular, in its isolated activity, is always the enemy of the whole, because it is precisely this whole which makes it feel its insignificance, or in other words, its limits.' On the state, Marx writes: 'The state permeates the whole of nature with cultural nerves, and at every point one must recognize that it is form, not substance, which is dominant; not nature without the state, but the nature of the state; not the servile object, but the free man.' Engels publishes several articles in the *RhZ* on the economic and political situation in England, on Chartism and the situation of the working class.

1843

The Ban on the Leipzig "Allgemeine Zeitung"
Self-Justification by the correspondent from the Moselle
Critique of Hegel's Public Law (P, 1927)

January–March: Marx continues the articles in which he attacks the Prussian censorship, and defends and comments on the reports published in November and December 1842 on the distress of the Moselle winegrowers. He is officially informed that, by government decision, the *RhZ* will be banned from April 1. The ban had been demanded by the Tsar following a violent article against Russian autocracy. Marx writes to Ruge (January 25): 'I can do no more in Germany, they are corrupting themselves (. . .) In the suppression of the *RhZ* I see a progress of political consciousness . . . It is painful to perform a servile task, even in the service of liberty, and to fight with pinpricks instead of with cudgels. I was tired of hypocrisy, stupidity and brutish authority, and also of kowtowing, manoeuvring, and having to employ a contorted, deceptive language.' In the same letter he alludes to a deep family conflict: 'I have fallen out with my relations . . . and while my mother is alive I shall have no right to my inheritance. Moreover, I am engaged, and I shall not leave Germany without my fiancée.' Disappointed by the timorous attitude of the *RhZ* shareholders, Marx resigns from the editorial staff of the paper, after maintaining (in comments intended for a memorandum to be sent to the government, in reply to the order banning the paper) that the policy of the paper had always corresponded to the true interests of the Prussian state. Marx, Ruge and Herwegh, the poet, plan to publish a new radical paper in Zurich. Marx to Ruge (March 13): 'As soon as we have signed the contract I shall go to Kreuznach and get married. Without any romanticism, I can tell you that I am head over heels in love and that I am very serious about it. I have been engaged for seven years and my fiancée has fought very fierce battles for me.'

March 13: Commenting on Feuerbach's *Thesen zur Reform der Philosophie* (1842) Marx writes to Ruge: '[Feuerbach] too often refers to nature and neglects politics. Yet the only way to transform contemporary philosophy into reality is through an alliance with politics.' (March 13)

End of March: Marx leaves for Holland where his mother's relations live. The reason for this journey is apparently the hope of obtaining his share of his father's legacy. The *RhZ* ceases to appear on March 31.

May: Marx goes to Dresden to discuss with Ruge the *Deutsch-Französische Jahrbücher* which they plan to publish abroad (Strasburg or Paris). In a letter addressed to Ruge from Cologne and published in January 1844 in the *Jahrbücher*, he violently attacks the Prussian monarchy and declares that 'the system of profit and commerce, ownership and the exploitation of men will lead . . . more quickly than the increase in population, to a rupture at the heart of present-day society which the old system will be unable to prevent, since it neither heals nor creates anything and does nothing but exist and enjoy itself . . . It is up to us to expose the old world and draw up a positive plan for the new one. The more time that events give to thinking men to become conscious, and to suffering men to unite, the more perfect will be the product born of those events and nursed by the present.' Marx settles in Kreuznach, the home of Jenny von Westphalen and her mother.

19 June: Marx marries Jenny von Westphalen. The Prussian government offers him the post of editor-in-chief of the *Preussische Staatszeitung*.

July–October: In Kreuznach, Marx works on a critical revision of Hegel's political philosophy which he had probably begun in March

1842. It is in this substantial manuscript that Marx breaks definitively with the ideas of the state as a rational institution. He states that in a true democracy the bureaucracy and the political state disappear, and that the Hegelian idea of a monarch incarnating the supreme political task reduces the state to an animal (zoological) existence. In addition he studies the history of the French Revolution (Ludwig, Ranke, Wachsmuth). Among his readings at this time, one should also notice: Rousseau, *The Social Contract*; Montesquieu, *l'Esprit des lois*; Machiavelli, *On the State*; T Hamilton, *Men and Customs in America*.

September: In a letter to Ruge, Marx sets out the programme of the new review: a merciless criticism of the established order in the name of a thoroughgoing humanism; participation in political struggles on the side of a form of democracy which would go beyond the framework of the political state; the reform of consciousness, not by socialist or communist dogmas, but by an analysis of the existing submerged consciousness, whether religious or political. As if to break with his political past as defender of an ideal state, Marx takes two works by Bruno Bauer as a pretext, and writes an essay in two parts, entitled 'On the Jewish Question.' He contrasts political emancipation which does not liberate man from the religious outlook, with human emancipation which will only be attained by doing away with the state and with money. In the first part Marx refutes Bauer's thesis that the Jews, like the Christians, should give up their religion: on the contrary; in a democratic state — such as the USA — freedom of religion as a political right is granted to all denominations. In the second part Marx denounces the Jewish religion, the source of Christianity, as a religion of Mammon and the cult of money. The essay will be published in Paris a few months later, in the *Deutsch-Französische Jahrbücher*.

October: Marx and his wife leave Germany and go to Paris (living at 38 rue Vaneau) where a group of Germans, among them A Ruge and G Herwegh, are already installed.

December: Marx becomes friendly with Heinrich Heine. He writes an essay, 'Critique of Hegel's Philosophy of Right', which, following the critique of the state and of money in 'On the Jewish Question' signals Marx's adherence to the cause of the proletariat; the liberating class, destined to 'realize philosophy', and obliged by a 'categorical imperative to overthrow all those conditions in which man is a debased, enslaved, abandoned, contemptible being.'

9

1844

An Exchange of Letters in 1843
On the Jewish Question
Contribution to the Critique of Hegel's Philosophy of Law. Introduction
Contribution to the Critique of Political Economy followed by a
concluding chapter on Hegel's Philosophy (P, 1932)
Marginal notes on the article "The King of Prussia and Social Reform"

January–March: The first and only instalment of the *Deutsch-Französische Jahrbücher* appears in Paris at the end of February. Besides the contributions of Marx and Ruge, it contains Engels' essay, 'Outline of a Critique of Political Economy'; Heine's 'Songs in Honour of King Louis'; 'Treason', a poem by G Herwegh, and Moses Hess's 'Letter from Paris'. Engels also contributes a review of Carlyle's *Past and Present*. Marx plans to write a history of the Convention.

April–June: Marx begins to study political economy and fills several notebooks with excerpts from his reading and lively comments on them. Within the year he will read French translations of the English economists (A Smith, D Ricardo, J Mill, MacCulloch); also Boisguillebert, J B Say, F Skarbek, S Sismondi, E Buret, W Schulz, etc. He makes contact with the *Ligue des Justes*, (a secret communist society founded in 1836) and attends workers' meetings. Relations between Marx and Ruge are broken off. The latter writes to Feuerbach (May 15): '[Marx] has a very distinctive character, that of a writer and scholar, but he is completely unsuited to journalism. He reads enormously, works with rare intensity, and possesses a critical talent which sometimes degenerates into extravagant dialectic; but he achieves nothing, he interrupts everything and ceaselessly plunges into a bottomless ocean of new reading.' However, Marx garners the first fruits of his studies in economics and begins to write a work in which he takes up the themes of the essay published by Engels in the *Deutsch-Französische Jahrbücher*. At about this time he outlines a critique of Hegel's *Phenomenology of Mind*, which he extends to the whole of alienated society, thus arriving at a humanistic ethic. Marx rejects the dialectical play of concepts: 'It is above all necessary to avoid postulating "society" once again as an abstraction confronting the individual. The individual *is* a *social being.*' He conceives this work as the first of a series of critical essays which he intends to publish as separate pamphlets and which will deal with law, ethics, politics etc., after which he will show, in a work of synthesis, the connection between the various parts.

July–December: Marx enters into contact with the editors of *Vorwärts!*, a German weekly journal, founded in Paris by Heinrich Börnstein. He has frequent meetings with Proudhon and their discussions, lasting long and late, seem to have been mainly concerned with the Hegelian dialectic. A little later Bakunin will join in these nocturnal conversations which only end with Marx's expulsion from Paris. In an article published in *Vorwärts!* and directed against A Ruge, Marx interprets the revolt of the Silesian weavers (June 1844) as a striking confirmation of the revolutionary spontaneity of the workers, which he contrasts with the political outlook of parties and governments. The parties seek power in order to exercise it at the expense of society: 'The existence of the State and the existence of slavery are inseparable.' Engels (who contributed to *Vorwärts!* between August and October a series of articles on 'The Situation in England') returns to the Continent and stops in Paris where he has long meetings with Marx. He has just finished his work on *The Condition of the Working Class in England* which will be published in 1845. Their community of ideas is such that they decide to collaborate in publishing a pamphlet, *The Holy Family*, against the coterie formed by Bruno Bauer around the *Allgemeine Literaturzeitung* (Charlottenburg). This pamphlet, to which Engels only contributes ten pages or so, will appear in Frankfurt-am-Main in 1845. From the outset Marx opposes 'real humanism' to 'German spiritualism' and declares the 'the proletariat cannot abolish the conditions of its own life without abolishing *all* the inhuman conditions of life in present day society, which are epitomized in its own situation'.

1845

The Holy Family or Critique of Critical Criticism
Theses on Feuerbach (P, 1926)

January to March: Under pressure from the Prussian government, Guizot, the Minister of the Interior, orders the expulsion of the principal contributors to *Vorwärts!* Before leaving Paris (February 3), Marx signs a contract with the publisher Leske of Darmstadt, for the publication of a work in two volumes, with the title *Critique of Politics and of Political Economy*. On the announcement of Marx's expulsion, Engels raises a subscription to help his friend 'in order that we should all share, in the communist manner, all the unwonted expenses that it will cause you . . . we must prevent these curs from having the pleasure of plunging you into pecuniary embarrassment as a result of their infamy.' In Brussels, where he will remain from February 1845 to March 1848, Marx resumes his studies in economics. During the whole Brussels period Marx fills about 15 notebooks with excerpts from authors both classical and critical. Among the latter, Sismondi and Baret occupy a prominent place. The history of political economy is represented by authors such as J Pecchio, J R MacCulloch, C Ganilh, Adolphe, Blanqui; the history of mechanics and technology by E Girardin, C Babbage, A Ure, P Rossi; monetary, banking and commercial history by T Cooper, T Tooke, J Wade, T R Edmonds, G d'Avenant, E Misselden, W Cobbett, G Gülich; demographic problems by M T Sadler, W Petty; socialism by R Owen, J Bray and F M Eden. During the same period Marx reads and annotates *Natural Law* and the *Analysis of the Economic Table* by Quesnay. Early in 1845 Marx writes a devastating critique of F List's *Das Nationale System des politischen Ökonomie* (1841).

April–August: Engels moves to Brussels; this is the beginning of a friendship and intellectual collaboration which will end only with Marx's death. The latter, who had at that time summed up his 'new materialism' in his *Theses on Feuerbach* (written down in a notebook), tells Engels of the 'materialist conception of history, worked out in broad outline'. The last (11th) thesis reads as follows: 'The philosophers have [only] *interpreted* the world in different ways: the point is to *change* it!' The two friends make a study trip to England. In London they make contact with W Weitling and the League of the Just; in Manchester they read a large amount of political economy. Marx brings back a notebook full of numerous excerpts from *Researches on the Principles of the Distribution of Wealth*, the work of Thompson, the cooperative socialist. In May, Engels' *Condition of the Working Class in England* is published in Leipzig. Observing the symptoms of crisis in the cities with high unemployment, Engels concludes that the war of the poor against the rich is imminent and that the communist revolution would be the most violent one.

September: Birth of Laura Marx.

October–December: Marx asks the Mayor of Trier for an emigration certificate for the USA, and asks to be released from his duties as a Prussian citizen. The Prussian government grants his request, Marx and Engels begin a joint work directed against Bruno Bauer and Max Stirner, author of *The Ego and Its Own* (1845). This manuscript contains the most elaborate statement of the critical and materialist concept of history. Marx gives up his Prussian citizenship (December 1).

1846

The German Ideology (P, 1932)
The Tribune of the People, edited by H Kriege

February-April: Marx and Engels take the initiative in founding a network of communist committees of correspondence; they contact G J Harney, the Chartist leader and editor-in-chief of the *Northern Star*, to which Engels has contributed in 1845 a series of articles on the political situation in Germany. At a meeting of the Brussels Committee of Correspondence, concerned with political propaganda in Germany, Marx violently attacks Weitling's sectarian communism and the philanthropic communism of the 'true socialists'. According to the account that Weitling gives to Moses Hess on March 31, Marx is said to have demanded a 'purge of the communist party['s]' contacts with 'financiers' and the abandonment of secret propaganda. 'For the moment, there is no question of achieving communism. First, the bourgeoisie has to take power'. According to Annenkov, who was also a witness to the discussion, Marx described as 'deception' any attempt to rouse the people without giving them solid bases for their action: 'In particular, to speak to the workers in Germany without having rigorously scientific ideas and a practical doctrine amounted to a dishonest and futile game, and a kind of propaganda which presupposed on one side an enthusiastic apostle and on the other simple fools listening with mouths agape.'

May: Marx invites Proudhon to join in the organisation of the committees of correspondence whose aim is to 'bring the German socialists into contact with the French socialists, to keep those in other countries informed about the socialist movements . . . in Germany, and to tell the Germans in Germany about the progress of socialism in France and

England. In this way, differences of opinion can be brought to light; there will be an exchange of ideas and impartial criticism. The social movement will have taken a step forward in its literary expression in order to rid itself of the limitations of *nationality*. And at the moment of action it is certainly a great advantage for everyone to be informed of the state of affairs abroad as well as at home.' In his reply (May 17) Proudhon agrees in principle to this proposal, while expressing some reservations about what he calls Marx's economic dogmatism. 'Let us not make ourselves the leaders of a new intolerance', he writes, 'or set ourselves up as apostles of a new religion, even if it is the religion of logic or of reason'. In his eyes, revolutionary action could not be a means to social reform. For him, the problem is to 'bring back into society, through an economic plan, the wealth which was taken out of society by some other economic arrangement.' Finally, he tells Marx of a forthcoming work in which he will set out his plans for reform. Marx and Engels draft a circular intended for the committees of correspondence in Germany, Paris and London in which they ridicule Herman Kriege, the 'prophet' of 'sentimental communism', who had emigrated to the USA and was publishing there a journal, the *Volkstribun*.

June–December: The network of committees of correspondence takes root in various regions of Germany and in Paris and London. The publisher Leske asks Marx to deliver at once the promised manuscript of the *Critique of Politics and Political Economy* or repay the advance. Marx explains the delay and promises to deliver the first volume by the end of November, arguing that before publishing his 'positive development' he felt it necessary to prepare the public by a polemical work against German philosophy and German socialism. Engels takes up residence in Paris in order to intensify communist propaganda among the German artisans. He sends Marx an account of his difficulties and also his criticism of Proudhon's book, *Système des contradictions économiques*, which was then in press. Marx loses no time in making himself acquainted with this book. His letter to Annenkov (December 28) contains a detailed criticism of it, which is to some extent a preamble to the riposte he will make to Proudhon in 1847. Birth of Marx's first son, called Edgar, after Jenny's brother, who is a member of the Brussels committee of correspondence. Having been unable to find a publisher in Germany for the bulky manuscript they had written between September 1845 and May 1846, Marx and Engels abandon *The German Ideology* to the 'gnawing criticism of the mice.'

1847

The Poverty of Philosophy
Karl Grün: The Social movement in France and Belgium
The Communism of the 'Rheinischer Beobachter'
Moralising criticism and critical morality . . . Against Karl Heinzen
Wages (P, 1932)

January-February: As Marx has not delivered the manuscript promised for November 1846, Leske informs him that the agreement made in February 1845 has been cancelled. At this time Marx is writing *The Poverty of Philosophy*. He deploys his talent as a pamphleteer, his knowledge as an economist and his political convictions, in this attack on Proudhon, once admired as the author of *What is Property?* The League of the Just sends an emissary (Joseph Moll) from London to Brussels to invite Marx and his friends; a reorganisation of the League is envisaged.

June: First congress of the Communist League in London, in which Engels participates. For lack of money, Marx is unable to attend. It is decided to reorganise the League of the Just and to prepare a communist declaration of faith for the next congress.

August: Marx is elected president of the Brussels 'commune' of the Communist League. With Engels he founds the Brussels *Society of German Workers*.

September: *The Westphälische Dampfboot* (a review of 'true socialism') publishes an essay, written by Marx in April 1846 in Karl Grün's book *The Social Movement in France and Belgium*. It contains a eulogistic reference to Proudhon's 'serial dialectic' in which Marx discovers a 'real relationship' with Hegel. In an article published by the *Deutsche Brüsseler Zeitung* (September 12) Marx attacks the anti-liberal and bureaucratic 'governmental socialism' of a Rhenish newspaper; he declares that the proletariat expects no help from anyone but itself. It prefers the rule of the liberal bourgeoisie to that of the bureaucracy, for the former provides it with new arms against the bourgeoisie, recognises the workers' party, and helps to promote it through the freedom of the press and of association. Marx is present at the free trade congress in Brussels (September 16-18). Being unable to obtain the right to speak, he writes out his speech and sends it to the press.

October–December: In a series of articles against Karl Heinzen, the advocate of a republican Germany constituted as a federation of autonomous countries, Marx asserts that the alternative is not 'monarchy or republic', but 'domination by the working class or by the bourgeois class'. At the same time he draws a historical picture of the backward development of the German bourgeoisie. As for the German workers, 'they know that their own fight against the bourgeoisie can only begin on the day when the bourgeoisie has triumphed . . . they can and should resign themselves to accepting the bourgeois revolution as a condition of the workers' revolution. But they cannot for an instant regard it as their final goal.' On November 9 Marx is elected vice-president of the *Democratic Association*, founded in Brussels on September 27. He goes to London on November 27, together with Engels, to participate in the 2nd congress of the Communist League. He is asked to draft, with Engels, a 'Communist Manifesto'. On November 29 at an international meeting organised by the *Fraternal Democrats* for the anniversary of the Polish insurrection of 1830, Marx and Engels deliver addresses. That of Marx ends with these words: 'Poland will not be liberated in Poland, but in England. You Chartists should not formulate pious resolutions about the liberation of nations. Defeat your own internal enemies and you will have the proud consciousness of having defeated the whole of the old society.' Marx meets the Chartist leaders Harney and Jones. After his return to Brussels he gives several talks to the Association of German workers on wage labour. Engels, on returning to Paris, writes a kind of 'Communist Catechism' comprising 25 questions and answers. When Marx later drafts the *Manifesto of the Communist Party* he relies heavily upon his friend's work.

1848

Discourse on the question of free trade
Manifesto of the Communist Party
Demands of the Communist Party in Germany
80 articles in the *Neue Rheinische Zeitung*

January–February: On January 9 Marx gives a lecture to the Democratic Association on the question of free trade, the text of which is published in February as a pamphlet. On his return from Paris, Engels tells Marx of his visit to Heinrich Heine (January 14). 'Heine has not much longer to live. I was with him a fortnight ago. He was in bed, having had a nervous attack. Yesterday he was up, but in a most wretched state. He can't walk three steps; he drags himself along and leans on the wall in order to walk from his armchair to his bed and back again.' On February 22 Marx makes a speech at a meeting organised to commemorate the Cracow insurrection of 1846. He emphasises the close connection that exists in Poland between the political and social problem and ends by declaring that the liberation of Poland has become 'a matter of honour for all the democrats in Europe'. Marx completes the drafting of the *Manifesto of the Communist Party*, after receiving a formal request from the central body of the association. The *Manifesto* is sent to London towards the end of January and is published there at the end of February. In this text of some twenty pages are to be found the central notions already developed in the *German Ideology* and *Poverty of Philosophy*. The future human society is here defined as 'an association in which the free development of each is the condition for the free development of all.' (MEW 4. p 482)

March: Marx receives from Flocon, in the name of the provisional government of the French Republic, an invitation to return to France. 'Brave and loyal Marx, tyranny banished you; free France re-opens its doors to you and to all those who fight for the holy cause of the brotherhood of peoples.' Almost on the same day (March 3) Marx is notified by royal decree that he is to be expelled from Belgium within 24 hours for having broken his promise not to engage in current politics. The next day, Marx is arrested and conducted to the French frontier, accompanied by his wife and children. They leave at once for Paris. Marx, with the powers delegated to him by the central body of the Brussels section of the Communist League, occupies himself with dissuading the German workers of Paris, and other democrats, from returning to Germany in the legion they have formed, 'in order to proclaim the German Republic.' At a public meeting Marx declares that the February Revolution is only the beginning of the European move- ment and that the imminent struggle between the proletariat and the bourgeoisie in France will decide the fate of revolutionary Europe. The German workers should therefore remain in Paris and get ready to take part in this battle.

End of March: Marx organises the return to Germany of members of the League and writes the *Demands of the Communist Party in Germany*.

17

This is printed as a tract and is distributed with the *Manifesto* to the workers returning to Germany. In the first clause of the *Demands*, Germany is declared 'a republic, one and indivisible.'

April: Marx, Engels and some other members of the Communist League leave Paris and go to Cologne where they immediately begin preparations for the founding of a big daily paper, the *Neue Rheinische Zeitung*.

May: Conflict between Marx and the commune of the Communist League, led by the physician Andreas Gottschalk who had also founded a workers' association. Gottschalk and his friends advocate the boycotting of the indirect elections for the national assemblies of Berlin and Frankfurt. It seems to be established that at this time Marx dissolves the Communist League, or at least temporarily stopped all propaganda activity, on the ground that since it is not a party of conspirators, there is no longer any reason for it in a country where the freedom of the press has been restored.

June: Publication of the first number of the *NRhZ*, 'the organ of democracy'; editor-in-chief, Karl Marx. In the course of 1848 Marx will write more than 80 articles, some of which extend over several issues of the paper, while Engels will contribute more than 40 articles. Marx is opposed to the federalist programme of the Left in Frankfurt and of the Radical-Democratic Party, and declares that 'German unity, like the German constitution, can only come from a movement in which the decision will result as much from internal conflicts as from the war against the East.' The 'revolutionary war' against Russia will become one of the main themes of the *NRhZ*; it will increasingly criticise the Left in the Prussian parliament, and the German bourgeoisie in general, which is frightened by the possibilities of the March revolution. In an article devoted to the 'June days', Marx praises the heroism of the Paris workers, and declares that the events in France 'have developed into the greatest revolution that has ever taken place, the revolution of the proletariat against the bourgeoisie.' (*NRhZ*, June 29).

July: Marx urges the liberals to make use of extra-parliamentary measures, and through a revolutionary war against Russia, to cleanse Germany of the sins of the past (July 5).

August: In the general assembly of the Democratic Association, of which he is one of the leading members, Marx takes up a position against the ideas propagated by W Weitling, who calls for a strong state power in order to resolve the social question. Marx stresses the importance of the mass political struggle, and in opposition to Weitling's programme he demands a 'democratic government composed of heterogeneous elements which must find the way to an effective administration through an exchange of ideas.' Marx takes part in the first congress of Rhenish democrats. Journey to Berlin where he has discussions with the leaders of the democrats and meets E Köppen and Bakunin. The Prussian government refuses to grant Marx citizenship, although the City Council of Cologne has approved his request.

September: Marx in Vienna where he attends the sessions of the Democratic Association. He gives a talk to the *First Workers' Association of Vienna* on the subject of Wage Labour and Capital. When the street battles in Frankfurt are announced (September 20) the *NRhZ* sets up a fund for the insurgents and their families. On September 26, following the proclamation of a state of siege in Cologne, the *NRhZ* is suspended for an indefinite period.

October: Marx takes over the leadership of the Cologne Workers' Association in the absence of Dr Gottschalk, who is in prison. The end of the state of siege having been proclaimed, the *NRhZ* reappears. (October 12)

November: After the triumph of the counter-revolution, Marx denounces the treachery of the German bourgeoisie and declares that 'there is only one way to shorten, reduce and concentrate the death-throes of the old society and the birth pangs of the new: revolutionary terrorism.' (*NRhZ*, November 7) The *NRhZ* leads a campaign to organise a tax revolt.

December: In a series of articles, Marx analyses the history of the Prussian revolution and pillories the German bourgeoisie. In his conclusion, he declares that 'in Germany a purely bourgeois revolution . . . is impossible' and that 'the only possibilities are absolutist-feudal counter-revolution or social–republican revolution'. The New Year article ends with these words: 'Here is the programme for 1849: a revolutionary uprising of the French working class; world war.'

1849

About 20 articles in the *Neue Rheinische Zeitung*
Wage Labour and Capital

January: At a meeting of the committee of the Workers' Association
Marx declares himself in favour of participating in parliamentary
elections on the side of the democrats and the opposition liberals,
'so as not to permit the triumph of our common enemy, the absolute
monarchy.' He conducts a similar campaign in the columns of the
NRhZ, against the 'Constitution bestowed from above', on the grounds
that bourgeois society by its industry creates the material means for
founding a new and free society, while the reactionary forces thrust the
nation back into mediaeval barbarism.

February: The *NRhZ* being accused of contempt of court, Marx pleads
his case before a Cologne jury. In his defence, which is both legal
and political, Marx reminds the jury of the threats to the freedom of
the press and of association in Prussia, and ends with these words: 'the
first duty of the press is to undermine all the foundations of the existing political state.' Marx is acquitted. The next day, he has to defend
himself again in the same court against the charge of 'incitement to
revolt' (refusal to pay taxes). He accuses the public authorities of
having violated the law, whereas the people had upheld it. No jury or
tribunal can judge a question which only history will solve. 'Society is
not based upon law. That is a legal fantasy. Instead, law must be based
upon society, must be the expression of society's interests and needs,
arising from the mode of material production, against the arbitrary
rule of individuals. I have in my hand the Code Napoléon; this did not
produce the bourgeois society, which emerged in the 18th century,
developed in the 19th century, and simply found it legal expression in
the Code. As soon as this no longer corresponds to social conditions it
becomes just a scrap of paper.' Marx is again acquitted. In two articles
entitled 'Democratic Panslavism', directed against Bakunin's *Appeal to
the Slavs* (*NRhZ*, February 15 and 16), Engels contrasts the sentimental and moralising romanticism of the Slav democrats with the historical
necessities which deny the right, to an autonomous national existence,
of certain peoples, such as the Slavs of Austria, who strictly speaking
have never had a history. For the Germans, hatred of the Russians,
Czechs and Croats is 'the pre-eminent revolutionary passion.' If need
be, the Germans will have to ensure the victory of the revolution in

alliance with the Poles and the Hungarians by means of 'the most resolute terrorism against these Slav peoples'. Marx is attacked by the Left in the Workers' Association who censure him for tactics contrary to the interests of the revolutionary party of the proletariat.

March: Marx announces that the *NRhZ* will celebrate the anniversary of the June Days and not the March revolution.

April–May: Marx leaves the Democratic Association and declares himself in favour of a congress of all the workers' associations of Germany. The *NRhZ* publishes in several articles the talks which Marx gave in Brussels in 1847 on *Wage Labour and Capital*. Any increase in wages in periods of capitalist expansion means enrichment of the capitalist class, while the working class is 'forging for itself the golden chains by which the bourgeoisie drags it in its wake.' (MEW 6, p 416) Marx travels to several towns in Germany to collect funds for the *NRhZ*. His article on the *The Deeds of the House of Hohenzollern* traces the history of Prussia, which owes its existence to treachery and violence as well as to servile submission to Russian despotism. On May 16 Marx receives a government expulsion order for having 'shamefully broken the laws of hospitality'. On May 18, publication of the last number of the *NRhZ*, printed in red. Marx's editoral sums up the general tendency of the paper by quoting certain phrases: to undermine the foundations of the existing order, a social republic, revolutionary terrorism, a social and republic revolution. The article ends by recalling the slogan of the first number on January 1, 1849: proclamation of a revolutionary war against Russia and the setting up of the 'red republic' in France. Marx makes a tour of various Rhenish towns in order to meet the deputies of the Left with a view to preparing for the insurrection which will protect the National Assembly.

June–August: Marx leaves Germany and goes to Paris where he makes contact with the secret workers' societies. On July 19 a government order confines him to residence in Morbihan. Marx's family (with three children and the faithful, servant, Hélène Demuth) is penniless. Lassalle comes to their aid by organising a subscription among their Rhenish friends. *La Presse* (July 30) publishes an open letter in which Marx declares that his only object in Paris is to pursue his scientific research. On August 24, Marx leaves Paris and goes to settle in London. His family will join him in September.

September: The central committee of the Communist League is recon-
stituted. Marx takes part in the relief operations organised for the
German emigrés in London.

October: Birth of Marx's second son, Guido.

November–December: Marx hears that a publisher in Hamburg is willing
to undertake the distribution of an economic-political review. The
contract will be signed in mid-December. Marx foresees a profound
commercial and agricultural crisis and fears a premature revolution on
the continent. On December 31 he attends a banquet of the *Fraternal
Democrats* at which the Chartist, G J Harney, presides.

1850

The Class Struggle in France
Articles and book reviews on various subjects in *NRhZ, Politisch-
ökonomische Revue*
Addresses of the central committee of the League (March and June
1850)

January: Avoiding contact with the German democratic emigrés,
Marx takes steps to ensure financial resources for the proposed review. He writes a preliminary essay, 'The Defeat of June 1848', the
beginning of a work in which he proposes to retrace and analyse
the history of the class struggles of 1848–49. He gets in touch with
the communist Röser in Cologne in order to set up – in view of the
existing conditions – secret communes of the League in the Rhine
province.

February–March: Marx gives talks on economic matters at his home to
several political friends. The first number of the *NRhZ P-Ö Revue*
publishes Marx's first historical essay and the first two chapters of a
work by Engels on *The Campaign for the German Constitution*. Marx
continues to work on *The Class Struggles in France* and, in collaboration with Engels, writes an economic and political 'survey'. Publication
of the 2nd number of the *NRhZ Revue* with the continuation of
Marx's study, 'The 13th June 1849' and the third chapter of Engels'
book.

March-April: With a view to the reorganisation of the Communist League, Marx and Engels send an Address to the communes, in which they sum up the 1848-9 revolution and define the tactics of the future proletarian struggle. They will aim at the autonomous political organisation of the proletariat and the creation of a workers' party 'both clandestine and public'. The Address advocates the establishment of revolutionary workers' governments in the form of municipal councils, and armed clubs, and workers' committees. With regard to the democrats, the proletariat will pursue a policy of vigilance and pressure in order to force the bourgeoisie to compromise itself, and to concentrate the maximum amount of forces of production, factories and means of transport in the hands of the state. The Address ends: 'The battlecry of the party of the proletariat will be 'permanent revolution'. Marx, Engels and Willich, as representatives of the Communist League, meet representatives of the Blanquist organisation (Adam and Vidil) and of the revolutionary Chartists (Harney) and decide on the formation of a 'Universal Society of Revolutionary Communists.' Article 1 of the Statutes declares: 'The object of the Association is the downfall of all the privileged classes and their subjection to the dictatorship of the proletarians, by carrying on a permanent revolution until communism is achieved. This must be the final form of the constitution of the human family.' Marx, Engels and K Schramm attend an international meeting to celebrate the anniversary of the birth of Robespierre. Engels and Schramm speak, the former exhorting the English to act in the revolutionary spirit of the Levellers, the latter defending the idea of the need for a workers' dictatorship as a preliminary to the abolition of classes. Publication of the third number of the *NRhZ Revue* with Marx's third essay 'Consequences of June 3, 1849' and the final part of Engels' study on *The Campaign for a German Constitution*. 'Finally', Marx says, 'the essence of revolutionary socialism is the idea of permanent revolution, and the dictatorship of the proletariat as a transitional stage toward the abolition of class antagonisms and the disappearance of the ideologies which express them.'

May: Publication of the fourth number of the *NRhZ Revue*, which contains an additional article by Marx on 'Louis-Napoleon and Fould' and reviews of books by Carlyle, Girardin, Chenu and La Hodde, etc.

June: A second circular to the communes of the League is issued (probably by the German section of the League) dealing with the situation of the communes in Belgium, Germany, Switzerland, France and England. The following deserves note: 'Among the French revolutionaries the truly revolutionary party led by Blanqui has joined us. The delegates of the Blanquist clandestine societies maintain regular and official relations with the delegates of the League of whom they have entrusted important preparatory work for the impending French revolution'.

July: Marx begins a systematic study of the economic history of the last ten years, after having received a reader's permit for the British Museum reading room.

August: Conflict between Marx and Willich about the attempts at reconciliation made by the organisations of democratic emigrés. Marx plans to emigrate to the US with his family and with Engels.

September–October: At a meeting of the central committee of the Communist League, Marx proposes the transfer of the League's headquarters to Cologne. To avoid a split, he suggests the constitution of two independent groups connected by a common central committee in Cologne. In justifying his plan, Marx condemns the revolutionary voluntarism of the group round Willich and Schapper. Marx receives a letter from the communists in Cologne urging him to publish a second edition of the *Communist Manifesto* and to finish his *Economics* with an eye to propaganda in Germany. At the end of September, Marx resumes work on his economic study which was planned and begun in 1844. At the British Museum he undertakes further reading (Mill, Fullarton, Torrens, Tooke; sets of *The Economist*; Blake, Gilbart, Garnier, etc.). In the 'survey' which they write for the last number of the *NRhZ Revue* Marx and Engels make a detailed analysis of the economic history of the last ten years and outline the social prospects for the immediate future. Their conclusion tends to show that a real revolution is impossible in a period of general prosperity; a new and inevitable economic crisis will be the preamble to the next revolutionary explosion. Marx, Engels and Harney formally break off relations with the 'Universal Society of Revolutionary Communists'.

November: Harney's *Red Republican* publishes the first English translation of the *Communist Manifesto*. Engels leaves London for Manchester where he will be employed until 1869 by Ermen & Engels, a firm of spinners in which his father is a partner. Publication of the last number (a double number) of the *NRhZ Revue* containing Engels' study *The Peasant War in Germany*.

1851

Collected Essays of Karl Marx (H Becker, Cologne)

A dramatic domestic event occurs at the beginning of the 1850s. Hélène Demuth, whom Jenny Marx has brought from Germany and who is nine years her junior, is about to have a son, Frederick Lewis, by Marx. The paternity is not recorded on the birth certificate. Engels is entrusted with the secret and will take responsibility for being the father. The few people who know of the event will keep quiet about it, at first out of respect for the family and later in order not to tarnish Marx's image, but it has subsequently been revealed, on the basis of reliable information, by W Blumenberg, *Karl Marx: An Illustrated Biography* (1962 English trans. 1972). Bert Andréas had made known the date and place of birth from official documents: 'Frederick Lewis Demuth, born June 23 1851 at 28 Dean Street, London [Marx's home]; died January 28 1929 as a retired mechanic.' Marx studies relentlessly during the whole year and fills 14 notebooks with excerpts taken particularly from the literature on money (S Bailey, H C Carey, W Clay, Joplin, S J Lloyd, W H Morrison, G W Norman, J Gray, J Francis, R Hamilton, D Hume, J Locke, J G Kinnear, P J Stirling, E J W Bosanquet, A Gallatin, J G Hubbard, W Leathan, C Raguet, B Torrens, T Twiss, etc.); on the history of civilisations (W Cooke Taylor, W A Mackinnon, J D Tuckett, H C Carey, etc.); on political economy (T Chalmers, G Ramsay, R Jones, T Hodgskin, MacCulloch, P Ravenstone, C P Scrope, R Torrens); industrial and workers' problems (J Fielden, P Gaskell, T Hodgskin, S Laing, N W Senior, J C Symons); agriculture and ground rent (J Anderson, T Hopkins, M de Dombasle, R Somers, E West, etc.); agricultural chemistry and population (J Liebig, A Alison, T Doubleday, J F W Johnston, Malthus, G Purves, R Vaughan, J Townsend); history of colonialism (H Brougham, T F B Buxton, T Hodgskin, A H L Heeren, W Howitt, H Merrivale, W H Prescott, E G Wakefield, J Sempère); history of Rome (Dureau de la Malle); history of the medieval towns and the fuedal system (J Dalrymple, J Gray, H Hallam, K D Hüllmann, F W Newman); banking (Bastiat, Proudhon, T Corbet, D Hardcastle, G Julius, C Coquelin, F Vidal); statistics

(A Quételet); technology (J H M Poppe, A Ure, Beckmann).

January–March: 'Marx lives in profound isolation; his only friends are J S Mill and Lloyd, and when you visit him you are met not by greetings but by economic categories.' (Pieper to Engels in January) In a letter to Engels (January 7) Marx sets out his critique of the Ricardian theory of rent; his friend confers upon him the title of 'The economist of groundrent' (January 29). A few weeks later, they exchange views on the theory of the circulation of money (February 3 and 25). Engels insists that Marx should finish his 'Economics' as quickly as possible. On February 24 the Willich–Schapper faction organise a great international banquet to commemorate the anniversary of the February revolution. The emissaries sent by Marx are abused and driven from the hall. Marx's financial situation becomes disastrous and Engels comes to his assistance. Birth of a fourth child, Franciska.

April: Marx sees an end to his studies and believes he can begin immediately to write his 'Economics', in three volumes. Thereafter he will plunge into another science. 'It is beginning to bore me. Fundamentally, this science has made no progress since Adam Smith and Ricardo.' (to Engels April 2) Engels, who knows his friend's appetite for reading, tells him how happy he is to see the work nearly finished at last. Publication in Cologne, by Hermann Becker, of the *Collected Essays of Karl Marx*. It contains articles which had appeared in the *Anekdota* and in the *RhZ* on Prussian censorship and the debates in the 6th Diet. Marx, now a communist, still wants his conceptions of radical democracy to be republished and diffused.

May–June: Lassalle, who has resumed his own studies in economics, burns with impatience to read Marx's 'Economics': 'this monster in three volumes from Ricardo turned socialist and the Hegel turned economist' (letter to Marx, May 12). Marx attends a lecture by Robert Owen. He learns of the arrest in Cologne of several members of the Communist League. German newspapers publish documents (circulars of 1850, Statutes of the League) found by the police on the arrested communists.

July–August: Johann Miquel, a member of the Communist League, informs Marx of the political consequences of the Cologne arrests. Material difficulties prevent Marx from working on his book. He reads Proudhon's *l'Idée générale de la révolution au XXme siècle* (The General Idea of Revolution in the 20th century) and plans to write a pamphlet about it, which 'will make him smart'. He sets out the broad outline in several letters to Engels. Charles Dana, editor of the *New York Daily Tribune*, invites Marx to contribute to his paper. At Marx's request Engels writes 19 articles on *Revolution and Counter Revolution in Germany* which will appear under Marx's signature in October 1851.

September-October: The German publisher, Löwenthal (Rütten & Löning) declines a proposal to publish Marx's 'Economics'. Arrest in Paris of members of the Willich-Schapper group. Newspapers attribute the seized documents to Marx, who publishes denials. He campaigns against the agitation of the German emigrés (G Kinkel, A Ruge, and A Willich).

November-December: Marx visits Engels in Manchester and discusses with him the plan of his three-volume work: a critique of political economy, socialism, and the history of economic theory. Exchange of letters with Lassalle on the political situation in France. Marx begins to write *The Eighteenth Brumaire of Louis Bonaparte*, a work intended for the weekly, *Die Revolution*, founded in New York by his friend, J Weydemeyer, who has recently emigrated there. Lassalle suggests the formation of a subscription society in order to publish the 'Economics', but Marx refuses this aid from the 'Party'; he does not want to expose his material difficulties to the public and he believes that the cowardly German bourgeoisie, trembling before Napoleon III, will not give him a penny.

1852

The 18th Brumaire of Louis Bonaparte
Great Men in Exile (P, 1960)
Some 10 articles in the *New York Daily Tribune*

January-February: H Ewerbeck sends Marx his book *Germany and the Germans* (1851) in which he praises the critical genius of Marx, who has drawn revolutionary inferences from the Hegelian dialectic. Ill and without funds, Marx can neither work on his book nor finish the *18th Brumaire*. Vain attempts by Marx to protest in the English press against the adjournment of the trial of the communists in Cologne.

March-April: In a letter to J Weydemeyer (March 15) Marx briefly defines his contribution to the theory of social classes; he claims to be the begetter of the conception of the dictatorship of the proletariat as a 'necessary' stage of transition to the classless society. The publisher Wigand (Leipzig) declines to publish Marx's 'Economics' for fear that it will be confiscated. Death of Franciska (April 14).

May-July: Publication of the *18th Brumaire* in the New York review *Die Revolution*. Half historical study, half political pamphlet, this work traces the course of events from 1848 to the *Coup d'état* of 1851, as France regressed from a bourgeois republic to a praetorian regime dominated by the theatrical and autocratic Louis Napoleon. Marx and Engels write a pamphlet, *Great Men in Exile*, a gallery of portraits which caricature the leading representatives of the German emigrés in London (Kinkel, Ruge, Heinzen, Struve, Meyer, Ronge, Goegg, etc.) The manuscript, sent by Marx to Bangya, a Hungarian officer, in return for a promised fee, will disappear along with Bangya himself, who is a spy in the service of several European police forces.

August-December: Marx writes several articles in German for the *NYDT* on the English elections of 1852 and the political parties in England, and Engels translates them into English. Marx proposes to the publisher Brockhaus a work on modern economic literature in England, but without success, and has equally little success with the publication in Germany of the *18th Brumaire*. Marx being in disgrace in Germany, the publishers are afraid of attracting enemies. The Marx family is in great distress: 'My wife is ill, little Jenny is ill, Leni has a sort of nervous fever. I cannot and could not call the doctor, having no money for medicines. For the last week I have fed my family on bread and potatoes, but I wonder if I shall be able to buy any today' (to Engels, September 8). Marx is informed by Bangya of Kossuth's attempts to win over Louis Napoleon to his plans, and he publishes these revelations in an article in the *NYDT* (October 19). He sends documents to the accused's lawyers in Cologne, publishes in the English press declarations on the vile deeds of the Prussian police and makes up his mind to write a pamphlet on the trial, which ends with severe sentences passed on most of the accused. On Marx's proposal, the Communist League declares itself dissolved (November 17). Marx writes to Engels (December 3) of 'Bonaparte's imperial honeymoons', the rise of joint stock companies, stock exchange speculations, the railway humbug: 'The sharp fellow is true to himself. The knight of industry and the pretender never contradict each other. If he doesn't make war, and quickly, he will be financially ruined. It's a good thing that Proudhon's rescue plans are realised in the only form which is practicable: as fraudulent credit and more or less direct swindling.'

1853

Revelations Concerning the Trial of the Communists in Cologne
History of Lord Palmerston (ed. 1899)
The Knight of the Noble Conscience
Some 60 articles in the *New York Daily Tribune*

January–March: The year 1853 may be considered as the beginning of that 'long night of exile' which will be henceforth the life of Marx and his family in London. The first three years of their life there, far from strengthening Marx's social, family and political position, are, on the contrary, profoundly unsettling. And his scientific reputation, confined to a small circle of the faithful belonging to the 'Marx party', has not allayed the fears of German publishers; after the trial in Cologne, Marx is considered the leader of an organisation of conspirators with international ramifications, aiming to destroy the Prussian monarchy and indeed all the European monarchies established by the Congress of Vienna. Whereas a year earlier Marx believed he was in the final stages of his preliminary researches, and that he would be able in a few months to announce the completion of a work in several volumes, he now resumes his abandoned studies and adds new notebooks to those, already numerous, of 1851, as if he still had a great deal to learn. But misfortunes combine to prevent him from continuing. Marx will abandon the work for four years, during which time he and his family are to plumb the depths of 'middle class poverty'. The contributions to the *NYDT*, which Marx soon writes directly in English, are devoted mainly to current political and economic events or are inspired by various occurrences which allow him, as historian and social critic, to deal briefly with more general subjects. The careful historical and statistical documentation in these articles is all the more evident in that Marx is most often exposing the inner workings of events; the pursuit of profit and thirst for power in the ruling classes, first of Victorian England and then of the great continental powers. For instance, when the newspapers report that a society of aristocratic ladies has protested to their American 'sisters' against negro slavery, Marx reveals that the president of this society is the Duchess of Sutherland and informs the American reader that the origin of the Sutherland family's fortune was the expulsion of Scottish peasants from the ancestral lands and their replacement by flocks of sheep. The articles ends with this phrase: 'The enemy of British wage slavery has a right to condemn negro slavery; a Duchess of Sutherland, a Duke of Atholl, a Manchester cotton lord . . . never!' (*NYDT* Feb 9) On the subject of the article in *The Times* which praises the exemplary effect of the death penalty, Marx denounces this glorification of the hangman, this *ultima ratio* of society, and he recalls the Kantian theory of law, defined by Hegel thus: the criminal has a right to punishment and ought to demand it. This idealism is only the metaphysical expression of the law of retaliation. And Marx quotes Quételet's statistics which show that the conditions of bourgeois society produce, with the regularity of natural phenomena, an average number of crimes. (*NYDT* February 18) The 2,000 copies of the *Revelations on the Trial of the Communists in Cologne* intended for distribution in Germany, are confiscated at the Swiss frontier, while another edition is published in a Boston journal (*New England Zeitung*). Marx accuses the Prussian government of having resorted to forgery and perjury, manufacturing missing documents, buying false witness and abusing the Laws of the Criminal Code in order to prove the guilt of the seven arrested members of the Communist League.

April–July: The Eastern Question fills Marx and Engels' correspondence. At his friend's request, Engels devotes a series of articles to this problem. The *NYDT* publishes some of them as editorials, others as contributions under Marx's signature. Marx plunges into the history of the East, particularly of India, where England is in difficulties. In his letters, he does not fail to point out that Russia will take every opportunity to push her expansion in Asia. Marx's study notebooks mention, among other authors, Stamford Raffles, M Wilks, G Campbell, R Patton, D Urquhart, J P Fallmerayer, C Famin etc. In addition, Marx has consulted a large number of diplomatic documents, drawn mainly from the publications of the *India Reform Association* and from D Urquhart's *Portfolio*. In an article on *British Rule in India*, Marx asserts that, in destroying the economic basis of the village communities in Hindustan, England, 'the unconscious tool of history,' is involuntarily bringing about a social revolution. (*NYDT* June 25) He later returns to this theme, declaring that bourgeois industry and commerce are creating 'the material conditions of a new world, in the same way as geological revolutions have created the surface of the earth. When a great social revolution shall have mastered the results of the bourgeois epoch, the market of the world and the modern powers of production, and subjected them to the common control of the most advanced peoples, then only will human progress cease to resemble that hideous pagan idol who would not drink nectar but from the skulls of the slain.' (*NYDT* August 8) Marx begins a systematic treatment of workers' problems in England, particularly strikes and their importance for the revival of Chartism. During the whole year he is in close touch with Ernest Jones, the Chartist leader, and is an active contributor to its journal, the *People's Paper*.

August-December: In a letter to Cluss, Marx writes: 'Scribbling for newspapers bores me, takes a great deal of my time, dissipates my energy and, to tell the truth, is worthless. Certainly it gives independence, but one is chained to one's paper and one's public especially when one is paid for each piece submitted, as in my case. Purely scientific work is quite another thing.' (September 15) He would like to know if an American review would consent to publish, and pay well for, a series of articles on the history of German philosophy since Kant. Charles Dana, editor of the *NYDT*, says he will find a review, but Marx will have to refrain from wounding the Americans' religious feelings . . . Nothing comes of it. From October to December Marx publishes eight articles on Palmerston in the *People's Paper*; some of them, reprinted in pamphlet form between 1853 and 1855, will be the most successful of Marx's writings, in terms of sales, but his name will be, as it were, brushed aside and he will apparently receive no money for them. In reply to the libellous attacks that Willich is spreading in the German press of New York, Marx writes a satirical pamphlet, *The Knight of the Noble Conscience*, published in New York in January 1854.

1854

More than sixty articles in the *New York Daily Tribune*

January-February: Essentially, Marx's correspondence with Engels and Lassalle and his articles in the *NYDT* revolve around the Russo-Turkish war and the consequences it entails for the western powers.

Marx, who wants the latter to intervene on the side of Turkey, will
judge statesmen, as in 1853, on the sincerity of their intentions and
the vigour of their actions against the Russian armies; that it to say,
against Tsarism, 'the last bastion of European reaction'. He discounts
an awakening of the revolutionary spirit in the popular masses, whose
apathy cannot be overcome by means of theory. One of the articles on
Palmerston, published in 1853, and distributed as a pamphlet by the
publisher, E Tucker, achieves a remarkable success. Marx meets David
Urquhart, an obsessive Russophobe, who compliments him on his anti-
Palmerston articles: it is as if a 'Turk' had written them, even though
the author calls himself a revolutionary (letter to Engels, February 9).
Marx denounces the Russophile attitude of Cobden, who has written
several pamphlets which vindicate Tsarism and its foreign policy.
(*NYDT* February 16) Using the information send to him under the
seal of secrecy of Lassalle, on the subject of Count Orloff's mission to
Vienna, Marx reveals that Russia's concern was to obtain the armed and
friendly neutrality of Austria. (*NYDT* February 21)

March–May: Lassalle does not share Marx's views either on the duplicity of France and England with regard to Turkey or on the role of
Palmerston; however, he agrees with Marx that the German revolution
will break out in a war to the knife against Russia. But it is fantasy
to hope that Prussia may form part of an alliance against the Tsar
(March 7). Marx is a delegate of honour to the Parliament of Labour
convened in Manchester by the Chartists. He sends a letter of congratulation in which he defines the task of this parliament, organised by
the working class with a view to 'the absolute emancipation of Labour';
the labouring classes have conquered nature, they have now to conquer
men. (*People's Paper*, March 18) Articles on the secret diplomacy in the
relations between England and Russia concerning the partition of
Turkey; English finances; the treaty of alliance between Prussia and
Austria, etc. Marx reads the *History of the Ottoman Empire* by J
Hammer-Purgstall. He informs Engels that the *NYDT* uses his best
contributions as editorials, and only publishes the mediocre articles
uder his signature (letter of April 22). In order to learn Spanish he
reads Calderon and Cervantes, and the works of Chateaubriand and
Bernardin de Saint-Pierre translated into Spanish. The *Republik der
Arbeiter*, a paper founded in New York by W Weitling, publishes a
series of articles (E Wiss, 'The Fundamental Trends of the Time')
against the 'economico-critical tendency represented in Germany by
Marx and those who blindly follow him . . . like Neptunists who think

the earth was created by the precipitation of the waters', they rely on the development of class antagonisms and on crises, and calculate the moment of revolution as one calculates the formation of geological strata. Marx draws for Engels a humourous picture of the author of this criticism, whom he calls 'a shareholder in Weitling's blissful stable'. (May 16)

June-September: Articles on the Crimean war, including one on the career of Marshal J Leroy de Saint-Arnand whom Marx describes as an unscrupulous adventurer and typical representative of the December gang. (*NYDT* June 24). Jenny Marx is ill and pregnant; the doctor demands his fees which Marx is not in a position to pay. '*Beatus ille* who has no family' (to Engels, June 21). On A Thierry's *History of the Formation and Progress of the Third Estate* (1853), Marx writes, 'It is odd that this gentleman, the father of the "class struggle" in French historiography, inveighs in his preface against the "moderns", as these also see an antagonism between the bourgeoisie and the proletariat and discern traces of it even in the history of the third estate up to 1789 . . . If M Thierry had read our writings he would have known that the decisive antagonism between the bourgeoisie and the people only begins, of course, at the point where they cease to be opposed as a third estate to the clergy and the nobility.' It is characteristic of the French bourgeoisie that it was constituted (and continues to develop) as a parliament and a bureaucracy, and not, as in England, by commerce and industry alone. In an articles in June on Austrian policy in the Balkans, Marx remarks, 'Austria has a narrow outlook; this miserable instrument in the hands of the Tsar and his English allies does not see that in this way it is preparing the elements of a universal revolution, of which it will be the first victim.' Marx is stimulated by the revolutionary events in Spain and begins to study them; until the end of 1854 he will send numerous contributions to the *NYDT* contrasting the 'semblance of war' of the western powers and a movement which in his opinion presages a revolution comparable with that of 1848. Marx compares Spain's feudal monarchy with Asiatic forms of government (oriental system of despotism). In 1854, Spain was not experiencing a social revolution in the modern sense of the word, the resources of the country being undeveloped and the sole national institution being the army, which for the people symbolised the state. At the same time, Engels sends Marx communications on the Crimean war in order to show that it is only a prelude to the great national struggles which will be recorded in the annals of 1855. At Marx's request (July 22) Engels signals Europe's powerlessness to resolve the Eastern Question and the belligerents' inability to carry on a real war: 'The fact is that conservative Europe — the Europe of Order, Property, Family, Religion — the Europe of monarchs, feudal lords and moneyed men, however they may be differently assorted in different countries — is once more exhibiting its extreme impotency. Europe may be rotten, but a war should have roused the sound elements, a war should have brought forth some latent energies; and assuredly there should be that pluck among two hundred and fifty million men, that at least one decent struggle might be got up wherein both parties could reap some honour, such as force and spirit can carry off from the field of battle. But no! Not only is the England of the middle classes, the France of the Bonapartes, incapable of a decent, hard-fought war; but even Russia, the country of Europe least infected by infidel and unnerving civilization, cannot bring about anything of the kind. The Turks are fit for sudden starts of offensive action and stubborn resistance on the defensive, but seem not to be fit for large combined manoeuvres without great armies.' (*NYDT* August 17)

October–December: In studying the recent history of Spain, Marx discovers in Chateaubriand, 'an aesthete of the pen, who combines in a most revolting fashion the Voltairian and aristocratic scepticism of the 18th century with the aristocratic sentimentality and romanticism of the 19th century.' In his *Congress of Verona* Chateaubriand, who had been sent by the Minister Villèle to avoid hostilities, openly proclaims himself the instigator of the war in Spain which only Russia approved (letter to Engels, October 26). Marx reads *The War in Mexico* by R Ripley (1849) and is struck by the portrait of General Scott, a mediocre soldier and a wretched diplomat (to Engels, December 2). Through the instrumentality of Lassalle, Marx becomes a correspondent for the *Neue Oder-Zeitung*, a liberal paper published in Breslau.

1855

Some 10 articles in the *New York Daily Tribune*
Some 100 articles in the *Neue Oder-Zeitung*

January: Marx begins his collaboration on the *NO-Z* with a retrospective article. He asserts that the English bourgeoisie has been obliged to accept the war against Russia under pressure from the people, and that the English aristocracy realises that from now on this war means the end of its monopoly of government. (*NO-Z* January 2). In most of his contributions to the *NO-Z* during January, Marx uses the articles that Engels has sent him and which he has forwarded to the *NYDT*. These articles deal mainly with England: military administration, the commercial crisis, the difficulties of the coalition ministry and the resignation of Aberdeen. Birth of Eleanor Marx (January 16). In leafing through the recent edition of the works of Heine, Marx notices that in a 'retrospective explanation' introduced in his *Französische Zustande* (1832) and dated August 1854, Heine relates how his honour had been defended by Dr Marx, 'his most radical and most intelligent' fellow countryman, against the calumny of a German newspaper; this had asserted, after February 1848, that Heine had sold himself to Guizot for a pension. 'The good Heine purposely forgets that my intervention on his behalf took place at the end of 1843 . . . In the anguish of his guilty conscience . . . Heine is trying to propitiate . . .' (to Engels, January 17). Marx gives Lassalle a summary of the effects of the abolition of the taxes on cereals in 1846. He concludes that, from 1849 to 1854, relative wages have fallen and from 1849 to 1852, profit has risen in relation to wages, which have remained stationary. (January 23)

February-April: The theme of the 16 articles in the *NO-Z* during February are the fall of the Aberdeen coalition ministry, the political parties, the Palmerston cabinet, the Crimean War, the state of the armies, Palmerston's political biography, and the death of Joseph Hume, veteran of the Commons. Marx refuses an invitation to an international banquet of emigrés to celebrate the February revolution: he does not want to expose himself unnecessarily to government persecution, nor to meet A Herzen, whose desire to see 'old Europe rejuvenated by an infusion of Russian blood' he does not share (to Engels, February 13). His contributions to the *NO-Z* during March deal with England's internal policy, the corruption of higher civil servants, the agrarian question in Ireland, the Crimean War, the strategy of the French general staff, the history of the Anglo-French alliance, the death of the Tsar as reported in the English press. From a letter to Engels: 'Some time ago, I re-read the history of ancient Rome up to the time of Augustus. The internal history really amounts to the struggle of the small landowner against the large, specifically modified of course by the system of slavery. Debt, which plays such a large role from the beginning of Roman history, only appears there as a natural consequence of small

property.' (March 8) Edgar ('Musch'), Marx's only son, becomes
seriously ill; after a temporary improvement, all hope seems vain: 'In
the end, the disease had taken the form of abdominal tuberculosis,
which is hereditary in my family . . . My wife has been in torment for
the last week. As for me, my heart bleeds and my head burns, but I
must bear up. Throughout his illness the child has not for an instant
changed his original character, agreeable yet independent.' (March
30) A few days later: 'Poor Musch is no more. He literally went to sleep
in my arms between 5 and 6 today. I shall never forget how your
friendship has lightened our burden during this terrible time. You
understand my grief. I have already had many kinds of ill luck but it's
only now that I know what real misfortune is . . . In the midst of all the
terrible suffering of these last days, I have thought of you and your
friendship, and I have been sustained by this as well as by the hope that
together we still have something reasonable to do in this world.' (April
12) For two weeks, Marx and his wife stay with Engels in Manchester.
After discussions with Marx who supplies the documentation, Engels
writes two articles on 'Germany and Panslavism' (*NO-Z* April 21 and
24). Panslavism is there defined as a movement which not only aims
at national independence but also strives to wipe out the results of a
thousand years of history. At the end of his article, the author
announces his intention of developing the subject by treating the
various forms of Panslavism which claim to be democratic and socialist,
Russian, etc.

May–July: The articles sent to the *NO-Z* during May deal with
England's political and economic structure, parliamentary debates,
leading politicians (Disraeli, Gladstone, Palmerston), Chartists opposed
to the Association for Administrative Reform, the Crimean War, etc.
These subjects will be taken up again in June and July in some 30
articles. In one of these contributions Marx comments on the Chartist
demand for universal suffrage and points out its historic significance:
'It is the People's Charter; it signifies their acquisition of political power
as a means of realising their social needs. In 1848 universal suffrage was
understood in France as a slogan of universal brotherhood, and it was
taken up in England as a battle cry. There the immediate content of the
revolution was universal suffrage. Here the immediate content of
universal suffrage is the revolution. When one studies the history of
universal suffrage in England one finds that it has become stripped of
its idealistic character, insofar as modern society has developed there
with the infinite contradictions that are produced by industrial

progress.' (*NO-Z* June 8) In his series of political pamphlets, Tucker publishes several of Marx's articles from the *NYDT* and the *People's Paper* on Palmerston. Marx continues to unmask the lack of breadth of 'Napoleonic ideas', especially the desire of the French emperor to reduce the war against Russia to the dimensions of a 'local war', whereas, according to him, the war could only be conducted on a European scale (*NO-Z* June 20). Marx attends a mass demonstration in Hyde Park organised to protest against the order closing shops and public houses on Sundays: 'In the 18th century the French aristocracy said: Voltaire for us. The mass and tithes for the people. In the 19th century the English aristocracy say: Bigoted phraseology for us, Christian observance for the people. The classical Christian saints mortified their own bodies for the salvation of the souls of the masses; our modern, cultivated saints mortify the body of the masses for the salvation of their own souls.' Marx denounces 'this alliance between a debauched, decadent and sensual aristocracy and the Church, which is supported by the sordid profit interests of a few big brewers and great monopolist merchants.' (*NO-Z* June 28). Marx to Lassalle: 'Bacon says that really great men have such diverse relations with nature and the world, so many things that engage their interest, that it is easy for them to forget the pain of any loss. I am not one of these great men. The death of my child has profoundly shaken my heart and my brain, and I feel the loss with the same intensity as on the first day. My wife too is completely broken.' (July 28) From July onwards Marx's signature disappears from the *NYDT* and his contributions are attributed to a *NYDT* correspondent.

August–December: Over a period of five months the *NO-Z* publishes some 50 articles by Marx and Engels in which they review the outstanding events of the time, both political and military. When Marx hears of the financial difficulties of the *NO-Z*, he suggests giving up his fees. Commenting on Lord John Russell's parliamentary and ministerial career after his resignation from office as colonial secretary, Marx writes: 'Placed by birth, connections and social accident on a colossal pedestal, he always remained the same *homunculus* – a malignant and distorted dwarf on the top of a pyramid. The history of the world exhibits, perhaps, no other man so great in littleness.' (*NYDT*, August 28) Having learned of the death of Roland Daniels, a friend of long standing, and member of the Communist League, Marx writes to his widow: 'He had a delicate nature, a refined and noble physique and a rare harmony of character, talent and beauty. Among the people in

Cologne, Daniels always seemed to me like the statue of a Greek god which a capricious chance had thrown among the Hottentots.' (September 6) In order to escape from the legal action brought by his creditor, Dr Freund, Marx stays with Engels for nearly four months. D Urquhart's *Free Press* reprints Marx's articles on Palmerston, first published in 1853, one of them as a pamphlet with the title *The Life of Lord Palmerston*. On the occasion of the publication of Admiral Charles Napier's correspondence with Graham, the Navy Minister, Marx recalls the careers of the two letter writers; he shows the corruption and anarchy prevailing in the British Admiralty, as revealed by the naval operations of the Crimean War: 'The best side of war is that it puts a nation to the test. Just as mummies decompose as soon as they are exposed to the air, so war pronounces sentence of death on all the social institutions that have lost their vital force.' (*NYDT* September 24)

1856

Revelations of the Diplomatic History of the Eighteenth century
Some 20 articles in the *New York Daily Tribune*
Several articles in the *People's Paper*
and the *Free Press*

January–April: In 1856 Russia's foreign policy is to be Marx's main preoccupation; he does his utmost to show the traditional submissiveness of English diplomacy to the interests of Russia. From December 1855 Marx frequently meets Bruno Bauer, who has been established in London for some months. Marx's old sparring-partner, from whom he had parted in 1843, has become an enthusiastic admirer of the East, and especially Russia, and he is very critical of the 'illusions' about working men and the class struggle (to Engels, January 18). Marx sends the *NYDT* several articles on the Danubian principalities and on Sweden, which are rejected by the American paper under the influence of an editor with Panslavic ideas (Gourovsky). At the beginning of February Marx makes some 'historic discoveries about the first decades of the 18th century and the end of the 17th century: they concern the struggle between Peter I and Charles XII and the decisive role that England played in this drama.' Marx summarises his thesis as follows: 'At that time the foreign policy of the Tories was distinguished from that of the Whigs quite simply by the fact that the former sold themselves to France and the latter to Russia.' (to Engels, February 12) Under Marx's influence, Engels begins a systematic study of the Panslavic movement and receives bibliographical information from his friend, accompanied by critical comments on the history and literature of the Slav peoples. (February 29) The delegate of a group of Dusseldorf workers informs Marx of the revolutionary atmosphere that prevails in the Rhine province, where the workers are only waiting for the signal of an insurrection in Paris, and the arrival of Marx and his friends, to go into action. Marx assures him that 'if conditions permit, we shall join the Rhenish workmen, but any isolated uprising without an initiative from Paris, Vienna or Berlin would be stupid; that if Paris gives the signal we must in any circumstances risk everything, even a defeat, which could only be temporary.' (to Engels, March 5) The same delegate reports to Marx on the activities of Lassalle, who is ambitious and vain and exploits the party for his own ends. Marx is sceptical about the revolutionary prospects in Germany, and is of the opinion that 'everything will depend on the possibility of supporting the proletarian revolution by a sort of second edition of the peasant wars.' (to Engels, April 16) Description of 'the France of Bonaparte the Small', which is in cruel contrast with the agonies of France at Cézanne, Lambessa, and Belle-Ille, and the France which perished in the Crimea. (*NYDT* April 14) Marx is the only foreign guest at a Chartist banquet organised to celebrate the fourth anniversary of the *People's Paper*. He delivers an address in which he predicts the emancipation of the proletariat, 'the secret of the 19th century and of the revolution of that century', an event heralded by the revolutions of 1848. Social revolution will owe less to revolutionaries such as Barbès, Raspail and Blanqui than to steam, electricity and the loom. Certainly, the victories of science seem to be paid for by moral defeats: to the extent that man subdues nature he seems to accept the oppression of man by man and the yoke of his own infamy. All the same, the new age has not only multiplied the number of machines; it has produced new men to master the new forces of society. 'Such men are the working men. The English working men are the first-born sons of modern industry. They will then, certainly not be the last in aiding the social revolution produced by that industry, a revolution which means the emancipation of their own class all over the world, which is as universal as capital-rule and wage-slavery.' (*People's Paper*, April 19) In several articles (*NYDT*, *The Free Press*, *People's Paper*) devoted to the fall of Kars during the Crimean War (November 28, 1853) Marx demonstrates, with supporting documents, that the defeat of Turkey was the result of the strategy imposed by the English government on the army commander, Stratford de Radcliff.

May-August: Jenny Marx travels to Trier with her daughters because of the illness of her mother, who dies on July 23. An article by Marx on Sardinia traces the history of the house of Savoy and speaks ironically of the rebirth of constitutionalism on Piedmontese soil after its failure in 1848-9. The article ends as follows: 'Once again the bourgeoisie is obliged to get support feom the mass of the people and to merge national and social emancipation. The Piedmontese nightmare is dissipated, the diplomatic charm is broken and the volcanic heart of revolutionary Italy begins to beat again.' (*People's Paper*, May 17) On the invitation of a German publisher Marx prepares to write a history of the secret diplomacy of the 18th century, and drafts the Introduction which he publishes in four parts in the *Sheffield Free Press* (June-August). In consequence of the cuts made in the text, and at Urquhart's insistence, the articles will be reprinted in their entirety in the *Free Press* of London (August 1856-April 1857) under the title *Revelations of the Diplomatic History of the 18th century*. Marx's well-documented study is both a savage indictment of the collusion between English and Russian diplomacy and an impassioned denunciation of the Tsarist policy of world domination, whose role Marx describes in these terms: 'It is in the terrible and abject school of Mongolian slavery that Muscovy was nursed and grew up. It gathered strength only by becoming a virtuoso in the craft of serfdom. Even when emancipated, Muscovy continued to perform its traditional part of the slave as master. At length, Peter the Great coupled the political craft of the Mongol slave with the proud aspiration of the Mongol master to whom Gengis Khan had, by will, bequeathed his conequest of the earth.' (*The Free Press*, February 25, 1857) In June, Charles Dana informs Marx that, as a result of events in the USA, the editors of the *NYDT* have been obliged during the past ten months to turn down 14 or 15 articles on Panslavism which Marx had sent, the subject lacking interest for the American public. In fact, Marx will learn from a reliable source that a member of the editorial staff of the *NYDT*, a Pole by the name of A Gourovsky, a notorious panslavist, had censored the articles in question, of which Engels was the author (to Engels, October 30). Among Marx's articles which appeared in the *NYDT* from June to August, and went beyond the mere provision of information, those on the Crédit Mobilier, and on the revolution in Spain are especially noteworthy. In the first, Marx arrives at a general evaluation of the role of joint stock companies which, as a factor in industrial development, have opened 'a new era in the economic life of modern nations' (*NYDT* July 11). In the second, Marx draws a lesson for the European bourgeoisie from the Spanish insurrections. From fear of the workers, the bourgeoisie will shelter behind despotism which it spurns; this is also the secret of the permanent armies in Europe. 'The next European revolution', the author concludes, 'will find Spain matured for co-operation with it. The years 1854 and 1856 were phases of transition she had to pass through to arrive at that maturity.' (*NYDT* August 18)

September-October: Marx writes for the *NYDT* a series of articles on the financial and commercial crisis, resulting from the fever of speculation which affected nearly all the capitals of Europe from September 1856 onwards. His favourite target is the Crédit Mobilier whose principal object is 'speculation for its own sake'. (*NYDT* October 9) One of his articles being a historical study of the problem of the circulation of money. (*NYDT* October 9) The Marx family (5 people) which has lived until this time in two rooms in Soho, now moves, thanks to a small legacy to Jenny Marx, to a villa near Maitland Park, in to a more airy district. Marx is studying the history of Poland and sends Engels an analysis of a work by L Mieroslavsky, *History of the Polish Commune in the 18th Century*. He notes that what has decided him to take Poland's side is the historical fact that 'the intensity and vitality of every revolution since 1789 can be measured with certainty by its attitude to Poland' (December 12). Marx is stimulated by the Prussian-Swiss conflict over Nauenberg to study the history of Prussia, and learns that this country's rise to power was due to 'mean thefts, corruption, direct purchases, impounding of inheritances, etc.' It is mediocrity in everything that has enabled this State to persist, 'exact book-keeping, fear of extremes, punctiliousness in military regulations, a certain primitive vulgarity and an ecclesiastical discipline. *C'est dégoutant*.'

1857

Against the Russophile pamphlets of Bruno Bauer
Bastiat and Carey (P, 1904)
General Introduction to the Critique of Political Economy (Grundrisse)
(P, 1903)

Principles of Economics (Grundrisse). Chapter on Money: chapter on Capital (P, 1939)
Some 50 articles in the *NYDT*
A few articles in the *Free Press* and *People's Paper*

January-February: Marx plans to write a pamphlet against the Russophile writings of Bruno Bauer, but this work is only begun. He reads *De la réforme des banques (On Bank Reform)* by A Darimon, a disciple of Proudhon, with an introduction by E Girardin. The author's admiration for Isaac Pereire moves Marx to this reflection: 'One can judge what socialist coup d'état Bonaparte still thinks he can resort to at the last moment.' (to Engels, January 10) The *NYDT* publishes only some of the articles sent by Marx and rejects the others. Among those published, several deal with the Anglo-Chinese conflict in Canton, the prospects for the Anglo-Persian war, the English elections in March, Russo-Chinese trade, etc. Marx is without funds after spending his last penny on the new house: 'I really don't know what to do, and in fact I'm in a more desperate situation than five years ago. I thought I had suffered the ultimate misery. *Mais non*. What is worse is that the present crisis isn't temporary. I don't see how I can get out of it.' (January 20) Marx foresees a possible break with the *NYDT* as soon as he has found another American paper. 'It is indeed sickening to be condemned to consider yourself lucky that such a rag will take you on board. Pounding and grinding up bones and making them into soup like paupers in the workhouse – that's what political work in this company comdemns you to.' (to Engels, January 23) On the manuscripts returned by the *NYDT* he discovers the hand of the censor, the panslavist Gourovsky. Dana promises to pay Marx for one article per week, whether it is printed or not, thus halving the fees of his correspondent.

March-July: Marx resumes his reading in economics, abandoned in 1852. He studies especially Volumes V and VI of Tooke's *History of Prices* which have recently appeared. His reading of the reports of the Factory Inspectors for 1856 provides him with subjects for two articles on the situation of factory workers and the factory system in England, which he illustrates with comparative statistics on the use of motive power in factories in 1838, 1850 and 1856. (*NYDT*, April 22 and 28) Charles Dana invites Marx's collaboration in an encyclopaedia in preparation (*New American Cyclopaedia*), especially for articles on the military art and military history. After consulting with Engels, who strongly encourages him, Marx accepts the proposal. Breaking a silence of nearly 18 months, Lassalle resumes correspondence with Marx and describes his solitary life in Düsseldorf, his travels in the East, the work he is about to publish in Berlin (*The Philosophy of Heraclitus the Obscure*) and a book on political economy which he hopes to finish in 1858. (April 26) Marx sends Lassalle's letter to Engels who advises his friend to answer him in order to obtain an explanation concerning his relations with the Rhenish workers' movement, but Marx does not answer Lassalle's letter. Charles Dana proposes that Marx should write the article on aesthetics for the *New American Cyclopaedia* in one page. Marx goes through F V Fischer's *l'Esthétique*, but does not write the article. In July Engels falls seriously ill and can no longer send articles to Marx. The latter will write the contributions to the *NYDT* until the end of the year, on the situation in China and India, the Anglo-Persian peace treaty, the role of the East India Company, the question of the Danubian principalities, and the economic and financial crisis. In addition, Marx writes a series of biographical articles for the *NAC* and a dozen articles on the Indian Mutiny of 1857. Jenny Marx has a still-born child. Engels stays at the seaside for several months to convalesce. In July, Marx sketches a critique of Bastiat's *Harmonies Economiques*; the preface is devoted to Carey whoe 'Yankee universality' he compares with the generalising mania of the French economist.

August–December: Marx studies the latest medical literature in order to diagnose Engels' illness and discover the treatment. The Eastern question again becomes topical and Marx writes an article for the *NYDT* in which he makes a close examination of the true motives for the policy of the various powers, especially in relation to the problem of the separation of the Danubian provinces from Turkey, and the unification of the principalities under the European puppet-prince. (*NYDT* August 27) In August Marx writes a *General Introduction* to his work on economics, in which for the first time he outlines the general plan, the logical and historical structure and the method of exposition of his 'Economics'. Anxious not to 'anticipate results he has not yet obtained', Marx puts this Introduction aside in 1859 and substitutes for it the preface to the *Critique of Political Economy*. After defining his own method in opposition to that of Hegel, Marx formulates the plan for his 'Economics', (in terms which are reminiscent of Hegel's logic of the concept) which precedes the 1859 plan, under six headings: Capital, Landed property, Wage labour, the State, Foreign trade, the World market (crises). In September and October the *NYDT* publishes eight articles on the Sepoys' Mutiny, the financial importance for England

of the Indian dominion and the role of the East India Company.
From October 1857 to the end of February 1858, Marx garners a
plentiful harvest of historical and statistical materials on the development of the economic crisis of 1857, which because of its international
dimensions seems to him the preamble to the collapse of capitalism and
the herald of a new revolutionary era. At the same time he presses on
with his theoretical work, and following the plan outlined in July he
writes 'the chapter on money'. In November, he begins to write 'the
chapter on capital,' on which he will work until June 1858. With regard
to the article on the Army written by Engels for the *NAC*, Marx writes
to his friend: 'The history of the army illustrates better than almost
anything our conception of the connection between the forces of
production and social conditions. In general the army is important
for economic development . . . Similarly, the division of labour *within* a
branch of production is carried out first in the army. The whole history
of bourgeois society is strikingly epitomised here.' (September 25) The
Marx-Engels correspondence from October to December is full of
exchanges of opinion and information on the various aspects of the
crisis, its revolution and its probable consequences. In concert with
Engels, Marx plans to publish in the spring of 1858 a pamphlet on the
crisis. Another letter from Lassalle; he reproaches Marx with his silence
and forwards a letter from Max Friedlander, the editor of *Die Presse* of
Vienna, who offers Marx the post of London Correspondent. Marx
receives *Heraclitus the Obscure* from Lassalle, and this time he replies:
he has always felt a great affection for Heraclitus to whom, among the
ancient writers, he prefers only Aristotle. As for his own work, Marx
declares that he had at last begun on the elaboration of the foundations
(Grundzüge) of his 'Economics'. 'I am obliged to work during the
day to earn my living. Only the night remains for real work, and I am
often troubled by illness . . . I cannot give you any news, for I am a
recluse.' (December 21) In a letter to Engels, Marx sums up the
conclusions to which his study of the crisis has led him, especially
concerning the situation of France. The crisis is not yet acute, but
French industry and commerce have been severely affected; the French,
characteristically prudent, have imposed restrictions on themselves
while accumulating enormous amounts of capital at the Banque de
France; closure of the Bourse; the real crisis only breaks out in France
after hitting Holland, Belgium, Germany, Italy, the Levant and Russia,
all countries with which France has an unfavourable balance of trade;
at the height of the crisis, the stock market will collapse and with
it the state, the principal gambler and speculator. Marx concludes

by giving Napoleon III very little chance of survival in 1858.

1858

Principles of Economics (Grundrisse) (continuation of the chapter on capital) (P, 1939)
15 biographical and historical articles in the *New American Cyclopaedia*
Some 60 articles in the *New York Daily Tribune*

January-March: Marx works, mainly at night, on his 'economic principles' and experiences difficulty with his arithmetical calculations. In desperation he begins to study algebra (to Engels, January 11). He makes discoveries: 'I have . . . overturned the whole theory of profit as it has been taught up till now.' Chance brings Hegel's *Logic* into his hands, and he makes use of it in his method of exposition. 'If ever the leisure for such work returns I should very much like to make intelligible to common human understanding (in a short work) the *rational* aspect of the method which Hegel discovered but at the same time mystified.' (to Engels, January 14) Marx's articles for the *NYDT* during the first part of 1858 concern the French crisis, British trade, the borrowings by the East India Company, the attempt on Orsini's life and the establishment of the 'rule of the Praetorians' in France, Pelissier's mission to England, etc. Lack of money in the Marx household, where there is no coal. 'If this situation lasts, I would rather be ten feet underground than continue to exist like this. Always to be a charge on others, while being tormented by the smallest worries; in the long run it is unbearable. I personally am free of the misery while I am working and continually thinking about general problems. But my wife, of course, does not have the same resources, etc.' (to Engels, January 28) Marx reads Lassalle's *Heraclitus*, and in a letter to Engels criticises its length, its pretentiously Hegelian manner, the parade of erudition, etc. 'I see from a note that our man plans, in a second *magnum opus*, to expound political economy in the manner of Hegel. He will learn to his cost that it is much more difficult, by means of criticism to bring a science to the point at which it can be set forth dialectically, than to apply an abstract and finished system of logic to vague intuitions of such a system.' (February 4) Three weeks later, Marx promises Lassalle to send him very soon his opinion of *Heraclitus*; he again makes a brief allusion to Hegel who was 'the first to understand the whole history of philosophy', even though he committed some errors of detail. In the same letter, Marx describes the difficult circumstances in which he is continuing and completing his economic writing. Could Lassalle find him a publisher in Germany who would be willing to issue the work in instalments? 'The work in question is, first, a critique of economic categories, or if you will, an analysis of the system of bourgeois economics. It is at the same time an analysis and a criticism of the economic system.' Marx cannot be precise about the length of the work in progress; he is afraid he will not be able, as he would have liked, 'to condense it, owing to lack of time, tranquility and money. The whole work is divided into six books: 1 Capital (containing some preliminary chapters). 2 Ground rent. 3 Wage labour. 4 The State. 5 International trade. 6 The world market.' Marx envisages a second work, a critique and history of political economy and of socialism, to be followed by a third, a historical outline of the development of the economic categories and relations (to Lassalle, January 22). The same day Marx writes to Engels: 'Fortunately, amusing things happen in the outside world. As for the private world, it seems to me that I lead the saddest life imaginable. So much the worse! There is no greater stupidity for people with wide-ranging aspirations than to marry and thus bind themselves to the trivial miseries of domestic and private life.' Exchange of letters between Marx and Engels on the problem of the depreciation of machines in relation to the cycle of industrial reproduction (March 2 and 5). Exchange of letters between Lassalle and Marx on the length and number of the various parts that Marx promises to deliver to the publisher. Marx wants to provide a first 'relatively self-contained monograph', the foundation of the whole work. He specifies the contents: 1 Value. 2 Money. 3 Capital in general (the process of production of capital, the process of circulation of capital, the unity of the two processes, or capital, profit and interest). He does not intend to construct all the planned six books in the same fashion, but to provide the foundations of the theory in the first three, while the last three would be limited to essentials, and would amont to five or six hundred pages in all. He estimates that the manuscript of the first part could be ready by the end of May (to Lassalle, March 11). Lassalle informs Marx that Franz Duncker, the publisher of *Heraclitus*, agrees to publish Marx's work and to pay good royalties. Letter from Engels on the shaky position of Napoleon III, whose imminent fall he foresees, preceded by a fatal economic crisis (to Marx, March 17).

April–June: Marx sends Engels the plan of his 'Economy' in six books (it is already known to Lassalle), detailing the contents of the first book which he divides into four sections: 1 Capital in general 2 Competition 3 Credit 4 Share capital ('the most complete form, culminating in communism'). Marx outlines the detailed plan of the first two chapters of the first section: 1 Value 2 Money. As for the third chapter (Capital) 'the most important in the first part', he is quite unable to say more at the moment because liver trouble prevents him from writing. (April 2) In May and June Marx sends the *NYDT* several articles on Disraeli's budget, the Franco-English alliance, the external trade and industrial pauperism of England, military despotism in France, the financial and fiscal systems in India, etc. From a letter to Engels: 'The movement for the emancipation of the serfs in Russia seems to me important as the beginning of an internal development in that country which could thwart its traditional external policy. Naturally, Herzen has discovered once again that "liberty" has emigrated from Paris to Moscow.' (April 29) Marx takes several weeks' rest with Engels in Manchester. He informs Lassalle of his liver trouble which has made him unable to work at his 'first part', and asks him to tell the publisher. With some reservations about certain details of *Heraclitus*, Marx praises the mastery and penetration with which the author has reconstructed the system of the Ephesian philosopher. (May 31) On the same day Marx writes to Engels: 'You will give me absolution for the praises I have had to accord to *Heraclitus the Obscure*.' Lassalle tells Marx about a duelling affair into which he has been drawn and asks for advice which would be consistent with 'the principles of our party'. (June 4) After consulting his friends, Engels and Wolff, Marx observes, while emphasising the irrational and anachronistic character of the duel: 'However, it is a feature of the narrowness of bourgeois society that in opposition to it certain feudal forms of individualism have preserved their right to existence . . . Individuals may find themselves drawn into such unbearable conflicts that the duel seems to them the only solution . . . In the present case, the duel would not have any meaning except as respect for a *conventional* form recognised in certain privileged classes. Our party must resolutely turn its face against these class ceremonies and challenge with the most cynical contempt the prententious demand to submit to it. The present circumstances are too important for one to engage in such childishness now.' (June 10)

July–September: Articles by Marx in the *NYDT* on the fate of the East India Company, the scandal of the illegal restraint of Lady Bulwer-Lytton, the increase in the number of mental patients, the suspension of the Bank Act of 1844, the crisis and the circulation of money, the history of the opium trade, etc. Pursued by his creditors, Marx tries to raise a loan and gives Engels a detailed account of his receipts and expenses. 'I would not wish my worst enemy to be plunged into the slough I have been in during the last two months, filled with fury to find my spirit crushed and my capacity to work destroyed by the extremes of misery.' (July 15) Marx tries in vain to persuade his mother in Trier to turn over to him in advance his portion of his father's legacy. In the autumn, his health restored, he works at his 'Economy' and counts on sending to the printer within two weeks the manuscript of 'two parts at once'.

October-December: The *NYDT* publishes, in the form of editorials and articles, Marx's contributions on Anglo-Chinese trade, British finances, Mazzini's recent manifesto, the abolition of serfdom in Russia, the madness of the king of Prussia and its consequences in internal and external policy, the regulation of the price of bread in France. From a letter to Engels: 'In view of the optimistic turn in world trade at this time . . . it is at least a consolation that the revolution in Russia has begun, for this is what I consider the convocation of the "notables" in Petersburg to be.' In the same letter, 'Properly speaking, the task of bourgeois society is the creation of a world market, at least in broad outline, and of the production based on it. Since the earth is round, this task seems to have come to an end with the colonisation of California and Australia and the opening up of China and Japan. The difficult question for us is this: revolution on the continent is imminent and it will at once take on a socialist character. Is it not bound to be crushed in this small space when in an area so much more vast the system of bourgeois society is still in the ascendant?' (October 8) Lassalle asks Marx for news of his 'Economy', not knowing what to say to the publisher, who is waiting for the manuscript of the first instalment. (October 22) Marx explains the reasons for the delay: illness, and scraping a living, but above all, his concern about the form, his style having suffered from his liver attacks. When it is a question of a book which has cost him 15 years of work and which propounds 'for the first time and in a scientific manner an important conception of social relations' it is vital that the form should be without blemish: 'I owe it to the party', Marx declares. He again writes explicitly that the 'first section' devoted to capital in general will include two parts instead of one (November 12). But in making a fair copy of the manuscript he sees the 'first part swell so much in the course of editing that it will finally include only the first two chapters: 1 Commodities and 2 Money, amd simple circulation. (to Engels, November 29) The 'third chapter' which is intended to contain 'das Eigentliche' (the essential core of the book) will not appear until eight years later, and will constitute the first volume of *Capital*, subtitled *A Critique of Political Economy*. The 'Part 1' of the 1859 will be incorporated in this volume, without the preface which sets out Marx's plan for his 'Economy' under six headings.

1859

A Contribution to the Critique of Political Economy Part I
Some 40 articles in the *NYDT*
Various articles in *Das Volk*, the *Free Press*, *Allgemeine Augsburger Zeitung* and *Die Reform*

January–March: The themes of Marx's articles published by the *NYDT* are the emancipation of the serfs in Russia, the question of Italian unity, the prospects of war in Europe, the situation in Prussia, the position of Napoleon III, factory legislation and industry in England. At the end of his contribution on the abolition of serfdom in Russia, Marx predicts a peasants' rising which will mark the beginning of a 'Russian 1793'. '. . . the reign of terror of these half–Asiatic serfs will be something unequalled in history, but it will be the second turning-point in Russian history, and finally place real and general civilization in the place of that shame and show introduced by Peter the Great.' (*NYDT* January 17) Marx ends the 'unhappy manuscript', but has not a penny for postage. 'I do not think anyone has ever written about money who was so lacking in it. Most of the authors who have dealt with it lived on good terms with the subject of their research.' (to Engels, January 21) He describes the plan of the work to Weydemeyer and observes that for political reasons he has decided to withhold Chapter 3 on Capital. But in the first two chapters, it is Proudhonian socialism, then in vogue in France, which will be demolished. 'I hope to gain a scientific victory for our party.' (February 1) Lassalle and Marx exchange views on the Italian complications and the possibility of a war between France and Austria. Marx enumerates the economic, military and diplomatic reasons which oblige 'the upstart in the Tuileries' to seek salvation in a warlike adventure. 'War', remarks Marx, 'will lead naturally to serious and, all things considered, revolutionary results,' while producing counter-revolutionary effects in its initial phase. (February 4) Engels tells Marx of his intention to write a pamphlet expounding the 'party's' point of view on the war which is brewing between France, the ally of Piedmont, and Austria. Marx immediately writes to Lassalle and asks him to find a publisher for this pamphlet, which must appear anonymously under the title *The Po and The Rhine*. 'You can be sure that the greatest military experts in Prussia will be suspected of being the authors.' (February 25) Lassalle succeeds in his approaches and informs Marx of this, at the same time sending him his most recent work, a drama entitled *Franz von Sickingen*. In a long letter he explains 'the tragic idea' of the play, or in other words 'the profound dialectical contradiction inherent in the nature of any action and especially revolutionary action.' (March 6) In three articles in the *NYDT* Marx paints a portrait of Napoleon III as a gambler driven by his past to solutions of despair and hence to war.

April–June: Articles in the *NYDT* on the effects of the financial crisis in India on the English domestic market, the war preparations of France, Piedmont and Austria, the financial panic in England, Mazzini's manifesto, etc. Marx sends Lassalle his appreciation of *Franz von Sickingen*. His principal criticism is directed at the artificiality of the characters in the play, who are simply mouthpieces of the spirit of the time; on the other hand he praises the author for having chosen as his subject the tragic clash between representatives of two classes, the knights and the princes. What the play lacks is a lifelike background which could only be provided by representatives of the peasants and the revolutionary elements in the towns. (April 19) This literary discussion between Lassalle on the one hand and Marx and Engels on the other will continue, to be replaced in June by a political controversy provoked by Lassalle's pamphlet *The Italian War and the Task of Prussia* in which Marx sees a justification of the policies of Napoleon III and the reactionary circles in Prussia. Lassalle's action will be characterised as a violation of 'party discipline', since for the party the revolutionary feature consisted in Prussia's participation on the side of Austria, involving a defeat for Russian diplomacy and thus for Tsarism, of which Napoleon III is the puppet. Marx expounds this point of view in several articles in the *NYDT*. Marx and Engels agree to help in the wider distribution of the journal *Das Volk*, the organ of the Cultural Association of German Workers in London, founded by the liberal publicist E Biskamp. They contribute several articles to this journal, dealing with the Italian war. In them Marx attacks Bonapartism, and those who lend themselves to the role of hostages and agents of Napoleon III, taking seriously his role as liberator of oppressed nationalities (Kossuth, Klapka, Vogt, etc.). Publication in June of the *Critique of Political Economy* Part I. In the preface Marx summarises his intellectual career and sets out the 'guiding thread' of his investigations, as well as the plan of the work in six sections, which he envisages as Capital, Landed Property, Wage Labour, The State, Foreign Trade, The World Market. Marx visits Manchester, where he collects funds for *Das Volk*.

July–September: Marx takes over the effective management of *Das Volk* in which, after the conclusion of the armistice of Villafranca, he resumes his criticism of Prussian diplomacy. At the same time, he sends the *NYDT* a series of articles on the results of the Italian war, and interprets the armistice of Villafranca as a retreat by Napoleon III in face of the threats of revolutionary movements in Italy and Hungary. He says that Napoleon is as completely unselfish as he is devoid of scruples; after spilling the blood of 50,000 men to satisfy his personal ambition, he is ready to perjure himself and to abandon all the principles he has hypocritically invoked, for whose sake he has led his men to a massacre. (July 28). Soon, in order to rehabilitate himself with his people, the Emperor will be forced to seek salvation in another adventure: to invade England or attack Prussia. Marx sends to *Das Volk* and the *NYDT* a diplomatic document which came to light in 1837 and was published by the *Free Press*: 'Russian memorandum for the guidance of the present Emperor', a document which expounds to some extent the philosophy of Tsarist expansionism. *Das Volk* publishes the first part of a study by Engels devoted to Marx's *Critique* . . . According to Engels, the work inaugurates 'an independent and scientific German political economy', as conceived by the 'German proletarian party', a political economy based upon the 'materialist conception of history' set out in the Preface, It is the first attempt since the death of Hegel to work out a systematic synthesis of a science, while transcending the speculative character of the Hegelian dialectic through a radical critique. Purged of its idealist trappings, the dialectical method applied to economics is, along with the materialist conception, Marx's fundamental discovery. Marx's articles published by the *NYDT* in August deal with the expansion of British trade, Napoleon III's blackmail of the King of Sardinia with a view to annexing Savoy, the rise in crime and pauperism in England in spite of the increase in industrial production and the expansion of its markets.

September-December: In his contributions to the *NYDT* Marx continues the examination of the significant economic and political problems of the time: the growing role of English financial capital on the world market, the relations between Kossuth and Napoleon III, the renewed Anglo-Chineses conflict, electoral corruption in England, the Franco-Austrian peace treaty of Zurich, etc. The Hungarian Szemere, a political emigré in Paris, informs Marx of the recantation of Kossuth who was Napoleon III's adversary in the autumn of 1858, but became a fervant partisan of the emperor a few months later and abjured his republican faith. Marx writes that it is no longer tolerable that the very men, who receive with one hand an assassin's pay from the French republic, with the other raise the flag of liberty; that they play two roles, as martyrs and as courtesans; that after becoming the tools of a cruel usurper they still make their appearance as representatives of an oppressed nation. (*NYDT* September 24) In his articles on the Anglo-Chinese conflict, Marx holds that, as in the two preceding Opium wars, one finds in this affair the hand of Palmerston, whose policy is directed to forcing the Asiatic states to make concessions to Russia. (*NYDT* October 1) With regard to the peace of Zurich, Marx defines the principle of the traditional diplomacy of the France of Richelieu and Napoleon III as follows: The first duty of France is to prevent the formation of powerful states on her borders and consequently to maintain at all costs the constitutions of Italy and of Germany which prevent national unity. (November 8) Talks on political economy to a 'chosen circle of work-men'. Marx to Lassalle, concerning the guarded silence in the press on the subject of his *Critique*: 'You are wrong... if you think I was expecting any eulogies in the German press, or that I set any great store by this. What I did expect was attacks or criticism, but not this total silence . . . These people have missed no opportunity to run down my communism so you would certainly think they might apply their intelligence to its theoretical vindication.' In the same letter Marx tells Lassalle the history of the Vogt affair which was triggered off by an anonymous tract published in *Das Volk* and reprinted by the *Allgemeine Zeitung* of Augsburg, denouncing Karl Vogt, naturalist and ex-member of the National Assembly of Frankfurt, as an agent in the pay of Napoleon III. (November 6) Vogt brings an action against the Augsburg journal and will eventually implicate Marx as author of the tract. Controversy with Freiligrath, whose unfriendly attitude with regard to his (Marx's) conflict with Karl Blind, author of the tract against Vogt, Marx condemns. The year ends without Marx having been able to deliver the promised continuation of Part I of the *Critique* to the publisher.

1860

Herr Vogt
Some 20 articles in the *NYDT*
Various letters and statements in *Kölnische Zeitung*, *Die Reform*, *Allgemeine Zeitung*

January–March: Marx will only be able to devote the first weeks of the year to his economic work; the Vogt affair and intermittent journalism absorb his time and energy. There will be, in fact, a noticeable reduction in the number of articles for the *NYDT*, some 20 contributions in all, dealing with Anglo-French and Franco–Prussian relations, the state of industry and labour in England, the Franco-Prussian alliance, the French intervention in Syria, Russo–Austrian relations, the reform of the Prussian army, British trade and banking. Marx pays close attention to the phenomena of crisis in the US and Russia and writes to Engels: 'In my opinion, what is taking place in the world now is on the one hand, the slave movement in America, set off by the death of Brown, and on the other hand, a similar movement in Russia. So the "social" movement is launched both in the West and in the East. This, together with the imminent collapse in central Europe, will be spectacular.' (January 11) Lassalle reminds Marx of his promise to deliver the next part of his work before the end of December. He says he personally is interested in its publication, as he also wants to being a 'systematic work on the same subject'. He has just read Vogt's pamphlet (*My case against the 'Allgemeine Zeitung'*) of which the first printing of 3,000 copies is already sold out. 'This pamphlet will do great harm to yourself and to the whole party, for it relies in a deceptive way upon half-truths . . . In short, something must be done.' More harmful than the scandal provoked by Vogt, it seems to him, is the presence in the party of W Liebknecht, who contributes to such a reactionary paper as the *Allgemeine Zeitung*. (January 27) Marx informs Lassalle that he will sue Vogt for defamation. As to his 'Economy', Lassalle would do well to wait for the 'second part' before beginning his own work. In it Marx will give the 'quintessence', but this will be only the conclusion of Book I, and there will be six books altogether. (January 30) Engels urges Marx not to let himself be diverted from his work by Vogt's libellous attack. 'In short, be a little less conscientious in your own work; it will always be too good for this miserable public. What is more important than anything is that the thing should get written and should appear; the inadequacies that bother you will never be discovered by those donkeys.' (January 31) In the following months, nearly all Marx's time will be spent in getting together documents concerning the case against the *Nationalzeitung* and the pamphlet against Karl Vogt. Marx's house will be transformed into an office for correspondence and records. The scientific work is still not abandoned entirely, at least in the early part of the year. In fact Marx feels 'If I apply myself to it energetically [my "Capital"] will be ready in six weeks, and once the trial is over, the book will find readers.' (to Engels, February 3) Marx goes to Manchester and discusses with Engels and W Wolff the plan of his pamphlet against Vogt. He mobilises his connections near and far to collect testimonials to his moral character, which are intended to demolish the edifice of Vogt's libels. In his controversial correspondence with Freiligrath, (a former communist and poet of the revolution, now a bank clerk), whose neutrality he does not forgive, Marx recalls their common past as militants of the Communist League, and explains the meaning of his action against Vogt: 'You, a poet, overwhelmed by toil, seem to misunderstand the full significance of the actions I have brought in Berlin and London. They are decisive for the historical claims of the party and for its future position in Germany.' And later: 'I tell you straight out that I cannot make up my mind to lose, as a result of trivial misunderstandings, one of the rare people whom I have loved as *friends* in the highest sense of the word. If I have committed a wrong against you, I am ready at any time to confess it. *Nihil humanum a me alienum puto.*' (February 23) When Freiligrath declares that he left the party after the dissolution of the League (1852) and that his poetic nature felt all the better for it ('the party also is a cage and one sings better, even for the party, when one is outside rather than inside') Marx replies, 'As regards the *"party"*, in the sense you speak of, I have known nothing of it since 1852. If you are a *poet*, I am a *critic* and I have had enough of the experiences of 1845-52.' For him, the party, in the 'ephemeral' sense of a clandestine or public society, has ceased to exist since 1852, and he is convinced that he serves the working class better through his theoretical work than in fighting in associations 'whose day is now over on the continent'. As for the League, like so many other societies, it has just been 'an episode in the history of the party, which springs spontaneously from the soil of modern society.' (February 29) A similar controversy takes place between Marx and Lassalle. It is envenomed by the dispatch of a confidential letter, which was communicated to Marx in 1853, in which Lassalle was painted in the most unpleasant colours. In a letter from Charles Dana, which Marx hopes to use in his law suits, as a testimony to his honourable character: 'Nine years ago I engaged you to write for the New York Tribune . . . You have written for us continuously . . . and you are not only one of the most highly-esteemed permanent contributors to our paper, but also one of the best paid. The only thing I have to reproach you with is that you sometimes emphasise too strongly your German feelings . . . This was the case regarding France and Russia. In my opinion, you have shown too much interest and concern for German unity and independence. This was perhaps more striking in the recent Italian war than on any other occasion.' (March 8)

April–July: *Savoy, Nice and the Rhine*, a pamphlet by Engels which is a continuation of *The Po and the Rhine*, appears anonymously in Berlin. In a contribution dated 'Berlin, 10.4.1860' Marx draws attention to the revolutionary climate which reigns in all strata of Berlin society (*NYDT* April 28). Lassalle sends Marx his latest publication (*Fichte's Political Testament*) and tells him about his current writing: 'I am working now on a big book. After that will come the political economy and three other works.' (April 16) The Attorney General of Berlin dismisses Marx's action against the editor of the *Nationalzeitung*. N I Sazonov, a Russian liberal journalist, whom Marx knew in his Paris and Brussels days, sends him a letter of sympathy regarding the Vogt affair, in which he writes: 'Your success is enormous among thinking men, and if you care to hear of the repercussions your doctrines have in Russia, I will tell you that in Moscow, at the beginning of this year, the Professor [I K Babst] gave a course of public lectures on political economy in which the first lecture was nothing more than a paraphrase of your recent publication.' (March 10) In connection with the Palermo rising, Marx writes an article for the *NYDT*, in which he describes the centuries-old struggles of the Sicilians against their oppressors both ancient and modern. (*NYDT* May 17) In another articles he echoes the rumours that Napoleon III is preparing for an imminent campaign on the Rhine. In a long letter to Lassalle, Marx sets out in detail the state of his court actions in the Vogt affair and explains his relationship with D Urquhart, with whom he has found himself in a 'cartel relation-ship' since 1853: subjectively Urquhart is romantic and reactionary, but objectively his activity in foreign politics is revolutionary. The Urqu-hartists have 'one great goal: a fight to the death against Russia and against the main support of Russian diplomacy, Downing Street in London . . . We revolutionaries must use them as long as they are necessary to us . . . The Urquhartists have never borne me any ill-will for having at the same time written under my own name in the *People's*

Paper, the Chartist paper of Ernest Jones, for which they have a deadly hatred.' In several articles for the *NYDT* Marx studies the development of British trade and industry and analyses recent factory inspectors' reports. (*NYDT* July 16 and August 24) Other contributions are concerned with the troubles in Syria and the French intervention there. (August 11 and 16)

September-December: After vainly attempting to find a publisher in Germany for his pamphlet against Vogt, Marx has it printed in London. Resuming their discussion on the Italian war, Lassalle tries to show Marx that events have proved him right, and he predicts a new Italian war for Venice in 1861 which would entail a revolution in Hungary. As for German-Russian relations, Lassalle completely agrees with Marx; war against Russia would be the most popular slogan in Germany, but such a war can only be fought *after* the revolutionary, since the German dynastic rulers are not capable of it. 'I consider war against Russia as our best and most necessary heritage. The war will help us to adopt a thoroughly revolutionary course, reduce our difficulties and make us capable of achieving real results.' (September 11) On the last point Marx replies to Lassalle that the opinion which he and Engels have of Russia is the fruit of long years of study of Russian diplomacy. 'It is true that Russia is hated in Germany, and from the first number of the *Neue Rheinische Zeitung* we have declared that a war against the Russians is Germany's revolutionary mission. But hating and understanding are two very different things.' (September 15) The two articles by Marx published in the *NYDT* in October draw attention to the consequences of domestic social problems for Russian foreign policy and return to questions of the policy in Prussia and France with regard to Italy. In November Marx studies England's financial situation and in a brief article comments on the effects of the rise in the bank rate in England on Napoleon III's financial policy. Jenny Marx has smallpox and Marx nurses her. He is unable to write anything. 'The only occupation which enables me to retain the tranquility of mind that is absolutely essential is mathematics.' (November 23) At the end of November, Marx reads the *Origin of Species* and writes to Engels that, 'in spite of its English ponderousness, Darwin's work contains the naturalist foundations of our ideas.' (December 19) *Herr Vogt* is published at the beginning of December. In spite of its character as a political pamphlet this last work contains numerous autobiographical and theoretical elements; it also outlines a fundamental critique of the Bonapartist and Tsarist trends in Europe in the second half of the nineteenth century.

1861

Some 12 articles in the *New York Daily Tribune*
Some 15 articles in *Die Presse*

January-April: Marx has just begun the second part of his career as a political figure and author in the shadow of a scandal. During the first part he has known distress and has been close to the abyss, but from now on, for the next ten years or so, his life is to be one of 'middle-class poverty': this euphemism is meant to indicate that his income will usually be about the same as that of a 'Manchester working man'. Ill and penniless, Marx makes vain efforts to persuade the German press to mention his *Herr Vogt*, an indictment of Tsarist Russia and its accomplices, Prussia, governed by William, the Prince Regent, and the France of Napoleon III. The papers, and Karl Vogt himself, pay no attention to this lampoon. As for Lassalle, while greatful to the author for 'the immense joy' that *Herr Vogt* has given him, he now declares himself convinced of the justice of Marx's accusation against the naturalist, but does nothing to broadcast this 'masterly work'. On the other hand, he tells Marx of his plan to found a journal in Berlin, and asks which of the old editors of the *NRhZ* would be willing to return to Germany for this purpose. Marx who has been asked by the *NYDT* to suspend his contributions for six weeks, would willingly have accepted Lassalle's plan, but does not believe that circumstances would lend themselves to such an enterprise. For relaxation he reads Appien (*On the Civil Wars in Rome*), which he likes very much. 'Spartactus seems the finest chap in the whole of ancient history. A great general (not a Garibaldi), a noble character and a real representative of the ancient proletariat.' (to Engels, February 27) In order to solve his financial problems, Marx visits Holland to see his uncle Lion Philips, who makes him an advance of £160 against his maternal inheritance. He then sets off for Berlin where for four weeks he is the guest of Lassalle with whom he discusses the new journal and the steps to be taken with a view to resuming his Prussian citizenship (renounced in 1845). He writes to his cousin, Nanette Philips, that Germany is a beautiful country, provided you don't live there. '. . . if I were quite free, and if besides, I were not bothered by some thing you may call "political conscience", I should never leave England for Germany, and still less for Prussia, and least of all for that *affreux* Berlin with its "Sand" and its "Bildung" and "seinen überwitzigen Leuten".' (April 13) In a letter to Lassalle, Jenny Marx writes: 'You give me great hopes of an early return to my country.

Frankly, I have lost it, this "dear" country. I have looked in every nook and cranny of my heart without finding a country there . . . Don't keep the Moor too long; I wish you every possible good, except that. At that point I become covetous, selfish and envious; all kindness stops and naked ineradicable selfishness begins.' (April) Marx meets his old friend of the *Doktorklub*, Karl F Köppen, 'still the same', but heavier and going grey, who gives him his book *The Religion of the Buddha and its Origin*. Marx is present, in a box reserved for the press, at a session of the Prussian second chamber, 'a curious mixture of civil servants' office and classroom', where alone among this 'stable of pygmies' and bureaucrats, a few men in uniform held their heads up (to Engels, May 10). On his return journey, Marx stops in Trier to visit his mother, who will not discuss 'ready money', but forgives him some old debts. 'For the rest, the old woman interested me by her shrewdness and the unshakeable evenness of her character.' (to Lassalle, May 8)

May-July: Marx hears that *Herr Vogt* has been put on the list of banned books in France. He makes contact with Simon Bernard, a French revolutionary, and formerly an intimate friend of Orsini, and with Ernest Jones, in order to organise a meeting in London to protest against the arrest of Auguste Blanqui. To console himself for his disappointments, he read Thucydides, 'The ancients, at least, remain forever new' (to Lassalle, May 29). At his request, Lassalle's friend, Baroness Hatzfeld, organises a press campaign in support of Blanqui who is being maltreated by the French police. Blanqui thanks Marx and 'the German proletarian party' through the intermediary of Dr Watteau (Denonville). Marx reads Lassalle's latest book *The System of Inherited Rights* and expresses criticisms which give rise to a discussion by correspondence between himself and the author. The Berlin Prefect of Police rejects his request for renaturalisation. In a comment on the reception of the 'Roman testament' through a 'misunderstanding' by modern jurists, Marx writes: 'The form which is misunderstood is precisely the universal form, admissable for general usage at a certain stage of social development.' (to Lassalle, July 22) Exchange of letters between Marx and Engels concerning the War of Secession in the United States. Marx sees the reasons for the conflict in the demographic and industrial preponderance of the North East region of the United States. Lassalle succeeds in persuading the publisher Brockhaus to look at the manuscript of Marx's 'Economy', suggesting that it should be published as an independent work, and not as the second part of the *Critique* . . . of 1859.

August–December: In spite of a few vain efforts, Marx's scientific work has been abandoned since 1859. While resuming his collaboration with the *NYDT* and writing for *Die Presse* of Vienna, Marx begins to write the next part of his *Critique* ... (1859), that is to say the chapter on the transformation of money into capital. The notebooks I–V (1861–62) along with notebooks XIX–XXXIII, written in 1863, are the first rough draft of Book I of *Capital*. (The notebooks I–V have been published in the new *MEGA* Vol. II 3, 1, 1976.) Marx spends about a fortnight with Engels in Manchester. Most of the articles sent to the *NYDT* and *Die Presse* between September and December are concerned with the Civil War in the USA and its economic consequences for England. Marx argues, first, that 'the struggle is between the highest form of popular self-government ever realised until now and the most abject form of human slavery ever recorded in the annals of history.' (*NYDT* November 7) Secondly, that the American government must at all costs avoid a conflict with England, which would benefit only Napoleon III. (*NYDT* December 25) Two articles deal with the intervention in Mexico, inspired by Palmerston, by France, England and Spain. (*Die Presse* November 12, *NYDT* November 23)

1862

Theories of Surplus Value (P, 1905–1910)
Some 30 articles in *Die Presse*
Several articles in the *New York Daily Tribune*
Third Chapter, Capital in General. I. The Process of Capitalist Production

As he had done in the *Critique*, Marx contemplates adding a historical supplement to the chapter on capital, such as he had outlined in his five notebooks of 1861, which would appear after the exposition of the theory of commodities, of money, and of surplus value. But this research will lead him much further than he had foreseen; during the year he will fill fourteen bulky notebooks (V to XVIII) of which only the last three (XVI to XVIII) deal with subjects which he will later develop in the third volume of *Capital*. The work will be frequently interrupted by illness and money worries. In March, Marx will have to end his collaboration with the *NYDT*, while *Die Presse* of Vienna will publish during the year only some of the articles sent to it. Aside from a few articles on the adventures of Napoleon III in Mexico, the Taiping rising, the economic situation and working conditions in England, Marx's contributions are concerned with the political and economic repercussions in England of the American Civil War.

January-March: In two articles, Marx expresses his admiration for the English workers who, although directly affected by the consequences of the Civil War in the United States, proclaim their attachment to 'the only popular government in the world' and rejoice at the peaceful solution of the *Trent* incident. (*NYDT* February 1) Such is the political influence of the working class that although it has no representation in parliament it forces the government, by means of public demonstrations, to abandon all idea of intervening against the American government. (*Die Presse*, February 2) Moreover, the English press is almost unanimous in its hostility to intervention, in spite of the blockade of the Southern States which paralyses the British textile industry. (*Die Presse*, February 4) After a silence of nearly two months ('my long silence has no "internal" reason; it comes of miserable circumstances with which I didn't want to bore or torment you.'), Marx tells Engels of his financial worries and informs him that his daughter Jenny is under medical observation: 'Jenny is already old enough (18 years) to feel all the burdens and all the misery of our existence, and I think this is the chief reason for her illness. Take all in all, it is not really worthwhile to lead such a lousy life.' (February 25) Engels, whose income has diminished significantly as a result of the American crisis, is obliged to reduce his standard of living. He sends Marx 14 bottles of wine. (February 28) *Die Presse* will receive an article on the advance of the Russians in Asia (occupation of an island situated between Japan and Korea), a fact about which the English press, 'Russified by Palmerston's influence', maintains a religious silence (to Engels, March 3 and 6). Marx uses for *Die Presse* some articles published by Engels in the *Volunteer Journal* on the Civil War in the United States. (*Die Presse*, March 27)

April-June: Several weeks' stay in Manchester. On his return to London, Marx finds his family head over ears in debt, and a letter from the manager of *Die Presse* asking him to send only one article each week in future. To Engels: 'Vico says in his *New Science* that Germany is the only country where a "heroic language" is still spoken. If he had ever had the pleasure of knowing *Die Presse* of Vienna or the *National-zeitung* of Berlin he would have abandoned this prejudice.' (April 28) In reply to Lassalle who is annoyed at receiving no reply to several letters, Marx writes, among other things, 'With regard to my book, it will not be ready for two months. During the past year, in order not to die of hunger, I have had to practise the most abominable trade and I have not been able to write a line of the "thing". Add to this my "idiosyncrasy": when I see in front of me something I wrote four weeks before, I find it inadequate and completely rewrite it. At all events, the book doesn't lose anything by this.' (April 28) In the same letter Marx recommends Lassalle to read Vico's *New Science*, and quotes some passages from the French translation (Paris 1844). Exchange of views between Marx and Engels on the military operations in the Civil War. Lassalle sends Marx copies of his recent addresses ('Fichte's Philosophy and the Significance of the German Spirit', 'The Nature of Constitutions', etc.) and the article written with Lothar Bücher, 'Herr Julian Schmidt, Historian of Literature'. He tells Marx of his intention to undertake some rapid reading for his economic work, which has been delayed but which he is certain to finish this time. He asks for the books by Roscher and Rodbertus which Marx had borrowed from him and hints at a journey to London in the near future. In his reply, Marx makes some comments, both complimentary and critical, on Rodbertus's *Social Letters* (concerning Ricardo's theory of rent) and refers ironically to the vanity and eclecticism of W Roscher. (June 16) Marx's financial situation is again desperate, and he unburdens himself to Engels about it: 'My wife tells me she wishes she were in her grave with the children, and I can't really blame her, for at the moment the humiliation, terrors and torments are intolerable.' Nevertheless, his scientific work is making better progress than ever, he will produce a large volume, since the Germans evaluate a book 'according to its cubic content'. He has completed the study of ground rent and has at last uncovered Ricardo's error. Reading Darwin again, in connection with Malthus's theory, suggests this comment to him: 'It is curious to find that, among the animals and plants, Darwin recognises his own English society with its division of labour, its competition, its conquest of new markets, its "inventions" and the Malthusian struggle for existence.' (to Engels, June 18)

July–September: On the occasion of the Universal Exhibition, Lassalle visits London and is the guest of the Marx family. From their conversations, which sometimes degenerate into real quarrels, Marx becomes convinced that, since their meeting in Berlin, Lassalle has passed from vanity to megalomania, to such an extent that the Marxes will regard him as an 'enlightened Bonapartist'. (to Engels, July 30) In the same letter, Lassalle's appearance is described in the most uncomplimentary fashion; Marx calls him a 'Jewish negro'. In two letters to Engels, Marx sets out his criticism of the Ricardian theory of ground rent, especially from the aspect of the organic composition of capital. He sums up his position thus: 'The only thing I have to demonstrate from the *theoretical* point of view is the possibility of absolute rent without violating the law of value. This is the point around which *theoretical* controversy has turned, from the Physiocrats until the present day. Ricardo denies this possibility, while I affirm it. At the same time I assert that his contesting it rests upon a theoretically false dogma inherited from Adam Smith: the alleged identity between cost prices and values of commodities.' (August 9) Marx makes a brief journey to Holland and to his mother in Germany in order to obtain some money, but fails completely. He applies for a post in a railway office, but is unsuccessful because of his bad handwriting.

October–December: In an article entitled 'Breadmaking' (*Die Presse* October 30), dealing with the replacement of traditionaly bakeries by industrial firms, Marx quotes the disclosures in an official enquiry into the poverty of bakery workers, and describes the mechanical methods of breadmaking. His article concludes: 'The triumph of machine-made bread marks a turning point in the history of large-scale industry; this is where the most strongly defended refuges of medieval methods are taken by assault.' (Marx will quote this report again later in *Capital*.) To avoid embarrassment with Lassalle over the repayment of a loan, Marx writes, 'I think that what is solid in our friendship will be able to sustain this shock. I confess frankly that, finding myself over a powder barrel, I have allowed circumstances to rule me, and this ill becomes a reasonable being. In any case, it was hardly generous on your part to bring against me, like a jurist or an attorney general, this state of mind in which I would have preferred to put a bullet through my head.' (November 7) This is to be Marx's last letter to Lassalle. (The latter, in the two years of life that remain to him, becomes immensely popular with the German workers.) Jenny Marx goes to Paris where she has discussions with the publicist M A Massol and with Elie Reclus with a view to a possible French translation of Marx's 'Economics'. Marx writes a long letter to Kugelmann about his work, which he says he has finished 'except for tidying it up and making the final revisions before it goes to the printers.' The volume will have about 500 pages, but although it is a continuation of the *Critique* it will be an independent work, having the title *Capital* and only as a sub-title *Critique of Political Economy*. In effect it will be Chapter III, 'Capital in general' as in the plan; without anything as yet on competition or credit. This continuation of the 'principles of political economy' will be the quintessence of the work which others besides himself will be able to develop, except perhaps for one thing: the relationship of the various forms of the State to the various economic structures of society. (December 28)

1863

Theories of Surplus Value (P, 1905-1910)
First version of *Capital*
Proclamation in Favour of Poland
The Polish Question (P, 1962)

Instead of turning to the actual writing of the continuation of the *Critique* . . . Marx continues his research on the theories of surplus value; he returns to his old study notebooks on the history of technology and attends courses on the subject. In a letter to Engels he sets out the problems raised by the relations between motive power, tools and machines in their historical evolution: 'For me it is the same with mechanics as with languages. I understand the mathematical laws, but faced with the simplest historical reality where intuition is necessary, I am in as much difficulty as the biggest imbecile.' (January 28) During the year Marx will add five new notebooks (XIX to XXIII) to the series begun in 1861. In an unpublished outline of Sections I and II of 'capital in general', the principal themes of the future volumes I and III of *Capital* are to be found.

January-April: Marx informs Engels of his wife's meetings in Paris (December 1862) with E Reclus and Massol who offer to translate Marx's forthcoming book. 'In Paris, the party spirit and a spirit of unity continue to prevail in the socialist party. Even people like Carnot and Goudchaux declare that a movement in the near future will carry Blanqui to power.' (to Engels, January 2) Engels tells Marx of the sudden death of his companion, Mary Burns. He receives his friend's condolences and at the same time, an account of his money troubles: 'It is terribly selfish to tell you about these horrors at this time. But the cure is homoeopathic, one misfortune makes one forget the other . . . In

the whole of London there's not one person in whom I could freely
confide, and in my own house I play the silent Stoic to balance the
explosions coming from the other side.' (January 8) Engels expresses
a passing irritation: 'You have chosen a fine time to demonstrate the
preeminence of your coldness of spirit. So be it.' (January 13) Marx
writes again to express his regret, and to depict the desperate situation
he was in: 'In such circumstances, I usually find no other refuge but
cynicism.' He intends to declare himself bankrupt in order to get rid of
his creditors, and to move into lodgings. (January 24) Engels; 'Your
last letter has obliterated the preceding one, and I am glad I have not
lost my oldest and best friend at the same time as Mary.' (January 26)
Not without risk, he obtains a sum of £100 for Marx. With regard to
Lassalle's *Workers' Programme*, which Marx calls 'a bad vulgarisation
of the (*Communist*) *Manifesto* and other ideas so often preached by us',
and in which the author claims to provide a 'philosophy of history' in
some forty pages, he writes to Engels: 'This fellow obviously thinks he
is the man chosen to be our heir.' (January 28) With the announcement
of the Polish insurrection, Marx sees a 'new era of revolution' opening
up under better auspices than in 1848, although enthusiasms and new
men are wanting. 'Moreover, we know the role played by stupidity
in revolutions and how it is exploited by the rabble . . . We must hope
that this time the lava will flow from East to West, and not vice versa,
to such good purpose that we shall be spared the "honour" of a French
initiative.' (to Engels, February 13) Marx and Engels decide to launch
a manifesto on Poland in the name of the Association of German
Workers in London; the part 'of military and political interest' will be
written by Engels, Marx reserving for himself the diplomatic part.
Together they collect an imposing quantity of historical materials and
Marx will make several attempts at writing. The return of his liver
trouble prevents him from giving definitive form to his drafts.

April–June: On the subject of a letter from Kugelmann, who insists that
Marx should devote himself principally to his 'Economy' and complete
it even though it does not deal with current affairs: 'These gentlemen
are not at all concerned about what I shall live on in the interim, while
I am doing this "non-current" work.' (to Engels, March 24) Engels:
'The good Kugelmann seems in fact to cherish the noblest plans for
you. It would be too prosaic, even an insult, for these good Germans to
imagine that men of genius also have to eat, drink, house themselves,
and indeed pay for all that.' (April 8) After reading again Engels' book
on *The Condition of the Working Class in England* (1845) Marx writes:

'On re-reading your book I have had a sort of regret at seeing myself grow old. What freshness, what passion, what visionary audacity in the way the question is grasped, without the prudent reservations of science and scholarship! And even the illusion that tomorrow or the day after tomorrow the historical outcome will burst into the light of day; all this gives the whole work a vivacious warmth and humour, in comparison with which "the grey upon grey" of later years appears devilishly disagreeable.' (April 9) Ill, disheartened and unable to work, Marx undertakes further reading on the history of economic theories. At the end of May he feels somewhat better and plans to get the 'Ecomony' ready for the printer and take the manuscript to Germany himself. 'If I could now retire into solitude, the thing would go very quickly.' (to Engels, May 29) The reading of Lassalle's recent writings ('Open Letter . . .', 'Indirect Taxes and the Condition of the Working Classes') places Marx in a dilemma: to retort or, by his silence, to provoke the author's anger. 'If I criticise his prose, I waste my time; besides he appropriates everything I say as his own "discovery". To rub his nose in his plagiarisms would be ridiculous, for I would not want to take responsibility for our ideas as distorted by him. One cannot praise this bragging and tactlessness either: Lassalle would immediately benefit from it.' (June 12) Marx wants to have done with his 'cursed book' as soon as possible, if only because Lassalle 'obliges us not to hide our light under a bushel this time.' (June 22)

July–December: Marx engages in mathematical studies (differential and integral calculus). He sends Engels the simplified plan of an 'Economic Diagram' which he has constructed on the model of Quesnay's *Tableau* with the intention of showing the 'process of reproduction as a whole' (July 6). From one of Jenny Marx's letters: 'My dear Karl has suffered a great deal with his liver this spring, but in spite of all the obstacles, his book is proceeding by giant steps toward completion. It would have been finished already if Karl had kept to the 20 or 30 printers' sheets envisaged. However, as Germans only have confidence in "fat" books, and as these worthy people have no taste for the subtleties of a concentrated style and the elimination of what is superfluous, Karl has added a great deal of historical material and it will now be a volume of 50 printer's sheets which will fall like a bomb on German soil.' (to Bertha Markheim, July 6) Marx continues with a fair copy of his manuscript and tries to give his work a 'tolerably popular form', to make it more comprehensible than the *Critique* . . . of 1859. While doing this, and in view of the mass of study notebooks on the doctrines of surplus value, much more voluminous than the rest of the strictly theoretical notebooks, Marx hopes to publish several 'large volumes'; in other words to make three books out of the three 'sections', and to reserve a fourth volume exclusively for the literature on surplus value. He meets the Pole, T Lepinski, an ex-colonel of the Hungarian revolutionary army, who has come to London to organise there support for the Polish insurgents. 'Undoubtedly the wittiest Pole-man of action though he is — that I have ever known.' (to Engels, September 12) Marx writes a proclamation on Poland for the Associa-tion of German Workers in England, in which he says: 'The Polish question is the German question. Without an independent Poland, there will be no unified and independent Germany; no emancipation of Germany from the Russian hegemony which began with the first partition of Poland.' On hearing of his mother's death, Marx goes to Trier where he settles the question of inheritance. On the way back he stops in Frankfurt to visit his aunts, and in Holland to see his uncle who is his mother's executor. There he falls ill (with boils) and for two months is looked after by his uncle and his cousin.

1864

Inaugural Address and Provisional Statutes of the International Working Men's Association
Address to Abraham Lincoln
Declaration against Karl Blind

January-April: During the first half of the year there is for the first time a marked improvement in Marx's financial situation, thanks to the legacy from his mother and a bequest from his friend, Wilhelm Wolff, who dies in Manchester on May 9. Exchange of letters with Engels on the Danish conflict provoked by the entry of Austrian and Prussian troops in Silesia. They estimate the chances of a revolution in Germany which alone could prevent the domination of Europe by Russia, who is directing the whole affair. On his return to London, Marx writes to his uncle in Holland. 'In spite of my carbuncles and my boils, I consider the two months I spent in your house as one of the happiest periods of my life, and I shall always be grateful to you for the kindness you have shown me.' (February 20) The Marx family settles into a more comfort-able home (1 Modena Villas, Maitland Park, Haverstock Hill). Marx, who is still afflicted with boils, stays for two weeks with Engels in Manchester. In a letter to Lion Phillips, he writes: 'You have difficulty in understanding Prussian policy: this comes solely from the prejudice of those who attribute serious and long range goals and plans to it. In fact, it is equally difficult to understand, for example, the Mormon Bible, since it does not actually contain a single spark of common sense.' The question of the Danish Duchies and the presence of Garibaldi in London lead him to believe that serious conflicts are developing in Europe: a rising in Austria, followed by a new Holy Alliance which 'would enable Napoleon le petit to play the Great. At this time, continued peace would be best, for any war delays the revolution in France.' (end of March) Marx rejects the Association of German Workers' request to participate in a deputation and write an address to Garibaldi (in whom he sees an accomplice of Palmerston). In a letter to his uncle in Holland, Marx summarises the ideas of Boethius (*De arithmetica*) and other authors on the method of calculation, especially division, used by the Romans; he adds some remarks on the unintelligibility of the universe resulting from the thoery of light. (April 14)

May-August: At Engels' invitation, Marx visits Manchester, where he is present during the last hours of Wilhelm Wolff. The latter leaves him £800 in his will. Reading Lassalle's *Capital and Labour* convinces Marx that the author is plagiarised his articles on *Wage Labour and Capital* published in the *NRhZ* Marx proposes to reprint his essay as an appendix to his forthcoming work, 'On some pretext, of course, without any allusion to Lassalle.' (to Engels, June 3) With regard to the Danish conflict in which Russia seems to desire the success of Prussia: 'The Russians have just taken an enormous step in the Caucasus. Europe, indifferent and foolish, has watched them take it. They must therefore close their eyes in that direction and they will do so willingly . . . These two affairs, the crushing of the Polish insurrection and the annexation of the Caucasus, are to my mind the two most important European events since 1815.' (to Engels, June 7) For several months Marx studies the Schleswig-Holstein question. He instructs Liebknecht on the attitude to take with regard to Lassalle's agitation. He and Engels leave him to follow his own course, but do not identify themselves in any way with his policy. Marx writes to Lion Philips that being prevented by illness from working he has speculated in American and English stocks, making more than £400, and he thinks of doing it again 'in view of the complicated political situation.' In the same letter, referring to the international Conference on the Danish question: he says: 'The only ones in this tragi-comedy who imperturbably pursue their old objectives and act in a masterly way are the Russians.' (June 25) To Engels: 'If I had had the money recently, I would have made a great deal. It is once again a time when with intelligence and very limited resources one can make money in London. (July 4) During his illness Marx studies physiology and anatomy. To treat his boils, he spends three weeks by the sea, at Ramsgate.

September–December: On receiving news of Lassalle's death in a duel, Marx informs Engels by telegram and Engels replies: 'You can imagine how this news has surprised me. Whatever his personal, literary and scientific worth, he was certainly one of the most remarkable minds in Germany. For us he was an unreliable friend in the present and an almost certain enemy in the future, but never mind: it is still sad to see Germany finish off all the men of the extreme radical party who have unquestionable ability.' (September 4) Marx to Engels: 'The Lassalle calamity has been on my mind for two reasons. In spite of everything he was from *la vieille souche* (the old family) and the enemy of our enemies (. . .) As regards the pretext for his death, you are absolutely right. It was one of those senseless acts which he committed so often during his life. With all that, I am sorry that our relations were unhappy in the last few years – though it was his fault to be sure.' (September 7) To the Countess Hatzfeld: 'He was one of the those men whose value I very much appreciated. For me it is all the more sad because our relationship had become less close in recent years . . . I know what the deceased meant to you. Be glad of one thing: he died young, at the peak of his triumphs, like Achilles.' (September 12) Marx is informed by W Liebknecht that J B Schweitzer and a group of workers want to entrust him with the direction of the General Association of German Workers. Marx declares that he is willing to accept on certain conditions. Marx is invited, as the representative of the German workers, to an international meeting at St Martin's Hall on September 28. He accepts, and proposes to his friend, J G Eccarius, the tailor, as spokesman for the Germans. In the course of this meeting it is decided to found an international association of workers. Marx is elected to the provisional Committee, with the title of representative of Germany, and is nominated as a member of the committee responsible for drawing up a declaration of principles and the provisional statutes of the association. He is ill and cannot be present at the first two sessions of this committee, during which drafts of the statutes are presented. At the following session Marx criticises these drafts, inspired by the ideas of Owen and

Mazzini. On November 1, he submits to the provisional committee his own texts of the Inaugural Address and the Statutes of the IWMA, which are unanimously approved. In the Address, Marx calls the Ten Hours Bill a victory of principles and of the 'political economy of the working class'. Recalling 'the immense and unresisted encroachments' of Russia, 'that barbarous power whose head is in St Petersburg, and whose hands are in every Cabinet of Europe', he exhorts the working classes 'to master themselves the mysteries of international politics . . . and to vindicate the simple laws of morals and justice, which ought to govern the relations of private individuals, as the rules paramount of the intercourse of nations.' Like the *Communist Manifesto*, the *Address* ends with the call: 'Proletarians of all countries, Unite!' The preamble to the General Rules of the IWMA declares at the outset that 'the emancipation of the working classes must be won by the working classes themselves' and that 'the economic emancipation of the working classes is . . . the great end to which every political movement ought to be subordinate as a means.' Marx meets Bakunin, whom he has not seen for sixteen years: 'I confess that I like him very much, and better than before. On the subject of the Polish movement he told me that the Russian government needed the movement in order to maintain calm in Russia itself, not realising however that the war would last for eighteen months. It therefore provoked this Polish trouble. Poland failed for two reasons: Bonaparte has influence there, and from the start the Polish aristocracy refused to proclaim peasant socialism openly and unequivocally. From now on after the Polish defeat, he (Bakunin) will participate only in the socialist movement.' (November 4) Liebknecht tells Marx and Engels of the nomination of Hermann Becker to the presidency of the Lassallean association, in accordance with Lassalle's last wishes. Marx agrees to cooperate with the *Social Demokrat*, the organ of the General Association of German Workers, directed by W Liebknecht and J B von Hofstetten. Sending the *Inaugural Address* to Kugelmann, Marx writes: 'I think that next year my book on capital (60 printer's sheets) will at last be ready for printing . . . I am afraid there will be an Italian–Austrian–French war next year, at the beginning of summer or in the middle of spring. This would be very damaging to the internal movement which is growing stronger in France and England.' (November 29) On the occasion of Lincoln's re-election as President of the USA, Marx writes an address for the Central Council of the IWMA: the first Declaration of the Rights of Man gave the 'initial impetus to the European revolution of the 18th century; the working class in Europe has understood that the rebellion of the slave owners was to sound the tocsin for a crusade of property against labour; past conquests are at stake as well as the workers' hopes for a new future.' Marx to Lion Philips: 'If you consider, my dear uncle, that 3½ years ago, at the time of Lincoln's election, it was only a matter of not making further concessions to the slaveowners, whereas now the avowed aim, already partially realised, is the abolition of slavery, you will admit that there has never been such a far-reaching upheaval. It will have the most beneficial effect on the whole world.' (November 29) At a meeting of the sub-committee of the Central Council, Marx criticises the francophile draft of an address in favour of Poland, by presenting 'a historically irrefutable picture of the permanent betrayal of Poland by the French, from Louis XV to Bonaparte III.' (to Engels, December 10) In letters to Leibknecht, Marx sharply criticises the cult of Lassalle in the *Social Demokrat*.

1865

Capital Volume III (P 1894)
Wages, Prices and Surplus Value (P 1898)
On Proudhon
Programme of the First Conference of the IWMA
Various statements, addresses, reviews

January–March: Marx attends regularly the meetings of the Central Council, whose debates turn on the support to be given to the Polish people, the position of the IWMA with regard to the various national working class movements and the dissensions among the members of the French section (Tolain, Fribourg, Limousin) some of whom are accused of Bonapartist inclinations. Visit to Engels and conversations with Ernest Jones. At the request of J B von Schweitzer and W Liebknecht, Marx writes an obituary note on Proudhon (who died in January 1865) for the *Social Demokrat*. 'You will see that certain vigorous blows aimed ostensibly at Proudhon fall on the back of our "Achilles" (Lassalle), for whom they are intended.' (to Engels, January 25) Marx declares that Proudhon's first book, *What is Property?* (1840) 'is undoubtedly his best work. It is epoch-making, if not for its new content then for its new and audacious way of saying old things.' Recalling his meetings with Proudhon in Paris, in 1844, he writes, 'In long discussions which often continued through the night I infected him, to his great harm, with Hegelianism, which he could not study properly because of his ignorance of German.' Finally, 'Proudhon inclined by nature toward dialectic. But as he never grasped the really scientific dialectic, he turned it only into sophistry.' He asks his friend to write an article for the *Social Demokrat* on the reform of the Prussian army. Exchange of letters with Engels on the subject of the treachery of Lassalle, who wanted to betray the workers' party to Bismarck in order to be recognised as the 'Richelieu of the proletariat'. (January 30) The publisher Meissner, of Hamburg, agrees to publish *Capital*. Engels stresses that Marx should take advantage of the favourable circumstances and finish the manuscript. At a meeting of the Central Council Marx pronounces himself in favour of the participation of the International in the movement for electoral reform in England (Cobden), on condition that the League's programme for reform should demand universal suffrage for the whole male population. At the same meeting, the reply sent by Charles F Adams, the American ambassador, in the name of Lincoln, to thank the Central Council for its letter of congratulation, is read out. Marx plans to reply to the libellous insinuations made by Moses Hess in the *Social Demokrat* against certain French members of the IWMA: 'the proletariat of Paris was and is utterly opposed to Bonapartism in both its forms, that of the Tuileries (Napoleon III) and that of the Palais-Royal (Plon-plon), and it has never for an instant dreamed of selling for a mess of pottage its historical birthright as a pioneer of the revolution. It is a model which we recommend to the German workers.' (to Engels, February 6) In a letter to J B von Schweitzer, Marx speaks of the importance of the syndicalist movement as a 'means of organising the working class in the struggle against the bourgeoisie', and criticises the Lassallean demand for workers' cooperatives financed by the state, as a system which extends governmental tutelage and corrupts the workers: 'It is absolutely beyond doubt that the fatal illusion of Lassalle (who expected a socialist intervention by the Prussian government) will be followed by disillusionment. The logic of events will tell. But the *honour* of the workers' party demands that it reject these fantasies before experience shows their futility. The working class is revolutionary or it is nothing.' (February 13) The *Social Demokrat* has adopted a policy of compromise in relation to the government; Marx sends a declaration, countersigned by Engels, to put an end to their collaboration with the paper. With reference to their ideas on 'Prussian governmental socialism', they recall the articles they published in 1847. Marx wrote at that time (with reference to the idea of an alliance of the proletariat with the government against the liberal bourgeoisie) that the domination of the bourgeoisie provides the proletariat with weapons, as well as with a position as an officially recognised party, to fight against the bourgeoisie. (*Social Demokrat*, March 3) In a detailed letter to Kugelmann, Marx sums up his relations with Lassalle and recalls their meetings in 1862 in London: Marx had shown that it was absurd to count on a 'socialist intervention from a Prussian state'; but Lassalle wanted to get the better of 'the realistic politicians', dictators of the proletariat, and use Bismarck as an intermediary between himself and the Prussian monarchy. (February 23) The Central Council adopts resolutions written by Marx with a view to moderating the conflict which had arisen in the Paris section of the IWMA, and to accepting as a member Citizen Pierre Vinçard, a Saint-Simonian song-writer and veteran of the 1848 revolution. Marx writes a brief review of Engels' pamphlet *The Prussian Military Question and the German Workers' Party*, published at the end of February. He quotes passages which exhort the Prussian bourgeoisie to fight for compulsory military service, 'the only point that interests the working class in Germany in the Prussian organisation of the army.' (*Hermann*, March 18) In a letter to Engels, 'Apart from the work for my book, the International Association takes up an enormous amount of my time, for I am in fact the head of this affair.' (March 13) Visit to his Dutch cousins. On his return, he finds the contract sent by the publisher Meissner, according to which Marx commits himself to delivering the complete manuscript of his work (in two volumes, amounting to 50 printer's sheets, ie 800 pages in total) before the end of May. Marx is appointed by the Central Council as provisional secretary for Belgium. Report to the Central Council on the strike of the Leipzig printing workers. Marx takes part in a movement to assist them.

May–August: Marx is suffering from boils and bilious attacks. Nevertheless he expects to finish his book within four months. After Lincoln's assassination, Marx is directed by the Central Council to write an address to the new President of the USA, Andrew Johnson. The address urges Johnson to continue the work begun by his predecessor. Irritated and provoked by a speech by the Owenite John Weston, a member of the Central Council, according to which a rise in wages is useless and trade union action ineffectual, Marx prepares a study on the question of wages and strikes, profit and surplus value, which he expounds at two meetings of the central council (June 20 and 27). For the first time, before a limited audience, he reveals some of the major theses to be presented eventually in *Capital*, notably the theory of surplus value. On the role of trade unions, Marx declares that they ought to strive to change the social system 'using their organised force as a lever for the final emancipation of the working class, that is to say, the ultimate abolition of the wages system'. He reads E Regnault *The European Question Wrongly Called the Polish Question* in which he becomes familiar with the idea (maintained by Duchinski) that the Russians are neither Slavs nor Indo-Europeans, so that in fact 'Panslavism in the Russian sense is an academic invention.' (to Engels, June 24) At Marx's instigation, the Central Council decides that the IWMA will not hold a congress in 1865, but only a conference, which will be convened in September 15 in London. Among the questions on the agenda are workers' struggles, the working class trade union and cooperative movements, the reduction of the working day, women and child labour, the Russian peril and the reestablishment of Poland, standing armies, etc. Having spent the money he inherited in 1864 and having received no income for more than a year, Marx is again without means and overwhelmed by debts. He thinks of betaking himself to Engels, but decides to continue his scientific work and to suspend for some weeks all participation in the work of the Central Council. In a letter to Engels: 'I assure you I would rather cut off my hand than write this letter. It's really depressing to depend upon other people for half of my life. The only thought that sustains me in this situation is that you and I are associates in an affair to which I contribute my time for that part of the business which concerns the theory and the party.' And concerning the stage he had reached in his scientific work: 'I have only to write three more chapters in order to finish the theoretical part (the first three books). After that I have to write the fourth book, the history of the literature, which is relatively the easiest part, since all the problems are solved in the first three books, the fourth being more a repetition of the other in a historical form.' At all events, he wants the work to form an 'artistic whole' before sending all the parts to the printer. (July 31) Engels' financial help is prompt, but Marx is tormented by his illness. His work hardly progresses at all, but his reading is not neglected: this time it is astronomy (Kirkwood and Laplace).

September–December: Marx is elected to the committee responsible for organising the IWMA Conference; he attends all the meetings of the Committee and of the Conference and frequently contributes to the discussions. He submits to the Conference a report of the preparatory committee on the agenda of the coming Congress, which is to be held in Geneva in May 1866. On the insistance of the French delegates, the question of religious ideas and of their social and political consequences is added to the programme prepared by Marx for the Geneva Congress. At a meeting of the Central Council, Marx pronounces himself in favour of a proposal sent by Polish emigrés with a view to celebrating the anniversary of the Polish insurrection of 1830 (October 17). Visit to Engels in Manchester. Marx receives from Berlin a letter signed by three workers which draws his attention to the artificial union between the General Association of German Workers and the German Workers: Party (it 'grafts Caesarism onto democratic principles'). They convey to Marx the desire of certain workers' circles to appoint him President Emeritus of the Association, and to see him take his place in a 'directory of three heads'. Financial difficulties oblige Marx to pass his days in trying to arrange his affairs, while keeping his nights for work: 'the International Association is such an incubus and everything relating to it weighs me down; I should be glad to be able to get rid of it. But it isn't possible, especially just now.' (to Engels, December 26)

1866

Speech on Poland
Appeal to the German Tailors
Resolutions of the Geneva Congress

January-May: During the whole month of January, Marx works, mainly at night, on the final text of *Capital*. In February, this overwork brings on a serious attack of carbuncles, accompanied by insomnia, and followed by rheumatism. A Proudhonist opposition group is formed among the French workers in London: this group follows the directions of Le Lubez and Vésinier, who are hostile to the Central Council and to its French members, whom they accuse of trailing in the wake of Bonapartism. Marx asks that Vésinier be excluded from the International. On Marx's proposal, Charles Longuet is appointed corresponding secretary for Belgium. Marx informs Kugelmann of the progress of the IWMA, especially in trade union circles and in the Reform League. 'As to my book, I work twelve hours a day giving it the finishing touches. I am thinking of bringing the manuscript of the first volume to Hamburg in March and visiting you on that occasion.' (January 15) Marx asks Engels to write a series of articles on the Polish question from the aspect of the interests and aims of the proletariat. Engels writes three articles entitled: 'Why is Poland of interest to the workers?' (*The Commonwealth* March 24 and 31, May 5). At a meeting organised to celebrate the anniversary of the Polish rising of 1863-64, Marx makes a speech in which, in the name of the IWMA, he expresses his workers' solidarity with the Polish people fighting for its emancipation. Confined to his bed and incapable of any theoretical work, he expands the section in *Capital* devoted to the working day by incorporating historical illustration, 'which was not foreseen in my plan'. (to Engels, February 10) Engels is very insistent that Marx should pay serious attention to his health, 'even if the book should have to be delayed for three months.' (February 10) 'If I had some money for my family,' Marx writes in reply, 'that is, a little more than nothing, and if my book were ready, it would be all the same to me if I were on the scrap-heap today or tomorrow, or in other words, died.' He explains the studies he has been obliged to undertake in order to complete the chapter on rent 'which in its present version constitutes almost a whole book' and further on: 'Although the manuscript (enormous in its present form) is finished, it could not be published by anyone but me, not even by you.' (February 13) Conflict in the Central Council with Luigi Wolff, a Mazzinian, and with the Germanophobe, Le Lubez. Marx has a holiday at Margate for three weeks. In a letter to Nanette Philips: 'During my enforced and prolonged absence from the Council of the IWMA, Mazzini has applied himself to fomenting a revolt against my leadership. "Leadership" is never a pleasant thing, nor one I covet. I always think of your father saying . . . that the donkey driver is always hated by the donkeys. But since I have embarked upon a venture I regard as important, "restless" man that I am, I should not like to give it up.' (March 18) On the tension between Prussia and Austria: 'The news from Germany is not very cheering. Prussia is urged on by Russia (and Bonaparte), Austria by the latter (rather unwillingly, in self-defence). Will our philistine bourgeois at last understand that, without a revolution which gets rid of the Habsburgs and the Hohenzollerns . . ., there is bound to be another Thirty Years' War and another partition of Germany!' (to Kugelmann, April 6) After an interruption of several months, Marx resumes his work on *Capital*. Exchange of letters with Engels on the Austro-Prussian dispute about the future of the Danish duchies.

June-August: Marx speaks at several meetings of the Central Council where the Austro-Prussian war is discussed. He criticises the point of view of the French (Lafargue, etc.) on the question of nationalities. 'The English certainly laughed when I began my speech by saying that our friend Lafargue, . . . who "has abolished nationalities", speaks to us in French, that is to say, in a language which nine-tenths of the audience scarcely understand. I also remarked that unconsciously he seemed to understand, by negation of nationalities, their absorption into the model nation, France.' (to Engels, June 20) Exchange of views with Engels on the Austro-Prussian war and the prospects of a Franco-Prussian war. Marx studies August Comte 'because the English and the French make so much fuss about this man. What fascinates them in him is the encyclopaedic aspect, the synthesis. But it is miserable compared with Hegel (although as a mathematician and physicist, Comte is superior in matters of detail; but even in this field Hegel is infinitely greater because of his universality).' (July 7) At a meeting of the Central Council Marx supports a resolution from K Brobczynski (Polish representative), which he had edited beforehand, on the necessity for workers to remain neutral and united in the conflict on the continent, which is a conflict between governments. The resolution is adopted unanimously. On August 6 Laura Marx becomes engaged to Paul Lafargue. Before the engagement becomes formal, however, Marx writes to Lafargue asking for 'positive information on his economic circumstances,' and continues, 'You know that I have sacrificed my whole fortune for the revolutionary struggle. I do not regret it. On the contrary, if I had my life over again, I would do the same. Only I would not marry. As far as it is within my power I want to save my daughter from the dangerous precipice where her mother's life was dashed to pieces.' (August 13) With a view to the Geneva congress, Marx draws up the instructions to the delegates of the Central Council in conformity with the programme adopted unanimously. To Engels, after Austria's defeat: 'Everything which centralises the bourgeoisie is, of course, advantageous to the workers. In any case, even if peace is concluded tomorrow, it will be even more provisional than that of Villafranca and of Zurich.' (July 27)

September–December: Formal engagement of Laura Marx and Paul Lafargue. Marx is re-elected corresponding secretary of the IWMA for Germany. In a letter to Kugelmann, he expresses his satisfaction with the results of the Geneva Congress and severely criticises the attitude of the Proudhonists who 'disdain all revolutionary action, which is born from the class struggle itself, and every organised social movement, which can therefore be achieved also by political means (for example, the legal reduction of the working day), on the pretext of liberty and opposition to government, or of anti-authoritarian individualism. These Parisians who for sixteen years have calmly endured, and still endure, the most miserable despotism, are in fact only preaching vulgar bourgeois science, embellished with Proudhonist idealism.' (October 9) It is Kugelmann to whom Marx also communicates the definitive plan of *Capital*, in four books, just as he had revealed it to Lassalle in 1858 (with the exception of Book IV): 1 The process of capitalist production; 2 the process of circulation of capital; 3 the forms of the general process; 4 the history of the theory. At that time Marx thought of publishing Books I and II in a single volume. When Engels hears that the first pages of *Capital* ready for the printer have been dispatched to the Hamburg publisher he expresses his great relief: 'At last then, a beginning of the execution, as the Penal Code says. I therefore drink a very special toast to your health. The book has done a great deal to ruin you; once you are rid of it, you will be quite a different man.' (November 11) Death of Marx's uncle, Lion Philips. (December 31)

1867

Speech on Poland (P, 1908)
Capital. A Critique of Political Economy Book I. *The Process of Capitalist Production*

January–April: Ill and suffering from insomnia, plagued by debts and threatened with eviction, Marx thinks of going to the continent in an attempt to improve his situation. Engels comes to his assistance. On January 22, at a celebration of the Polish insurrection of 1863-1864 Marx makes an inflammatory speech against Russia, which he accuses of aiming at world domination by the most diverse means and tactics. To achieve this aim it has to make Poland into its pliable instrument. 'There is only one alternative left for Europe. Asiatic barbarism under Muscovite leadership will burst over her head like a lawine (sic!) or she must restore Poland, thus placing between her and Asia, 20 million heroes and gaining breathing time for the accomplishment of her social regeneration.' Talk on wage labour and capital to the Cultural Association of German Workers in London (February 28): 'The so-called free worker is certainly conscious of being a free worker, but he is all the more at the mercy of the power of capital because he is obliged to sell his labour for a miserable wage, and thus receives in exchange only the minimum required to support life.' Marx concludes by speaking of the radical vocation of the German proletariat which will not need to pass through the stage of a bourgeois movement. 'It will be forced by its geographical situation to declare war on oriental barbarism, for it is from Asia that the whole reaction against the West has come. It is in this way that the workers' party will be drawn into the revolutionary arena, where it will act to liberate itself completely.' (Review in *Der Verbote*, March 3) Marx completes the final revision of *Capital* (Book I), and thanks to financial help from Engels, travels to Hamburg in order to deliver the manuscript to the publisher himself. He stays with Kugelmann in Hanover. He informs J P Becker of the object of his journey and asks him to announce in the press that his book is about to be published: 'It is certainly the most terrible missile that has ever been hurled at the head of the bourgeoisie (land-owners included).' (April 17) Kugelmann, a well-known gynaecologist, 'is a fanatical adherent of ou doctrine and of ourselves ... He possesses a collection of our works which is better than the one we have. I found in it *The Holy Family*, which he presented to me, and he is also sending you a copy.' In the same letter: 'Bismarck has chosen me as one of his satraps. He wants to use me, and my great talents, in the interests of the German people.' (to Engels, April 24) To a German socialist who had emigrated to the United State he writes: 'Why haven't I answered you? Because I have been continually at death's door. I therefore had to take advantage of *every* instant when I was well in order to finish my book, to which I have sacrificed health, happiness and family. I hope that this statement will not provoke any comment. I despise so-called "practical" people and their wisdom. If one chose to be a brute one could of course turn one's back on human suffering and look after one's own interests. But I should really have been very unpractical if I had died without finishing my book, even if only in manuscript.' (April 30)

May–July: Marx writes to Ludwig Büchner, a natural scientist in Darmstadt, whose book *Force and Matter* had been published in French, to ask him for the name of a translator for *Capital*: 'I believe it is of the greatest importance to liberate the French from the false ideas in which Proudhon has imprisoned them with his petty-bourgeois idealist mentality. At the recent Congress in Geneva, as in the relations I have with the French branch as a member of the Council of the IWMA, one is constantly coming up against the most repugnant consequences of Proudhonism.' (May 1) The publisher Meissner insists on Marx sending him Book II of *Capital* by autumn at the latest. Marx is convinced that he is at a turning point in his career and that his material situation will now be permanently secure. 'Without you,' he writes to Engels, 'I should never have been able to bring the book to a successful issue, and I assure you that I have a burden on my conscience, for I know that it is mainly on my account that you have squandered your remarkable energies and let them rust away in commerce; and that into the bargain you have shared in all my little troubles.' (May 7) Engels regularly reads the proofs of *Capital* and tells Marx what he thinks of them. He criticises the presentation of certain parts which are not sufficiently divided up and spaced out by sub-titles, and he discovers in some pages 'traces of the carbuncles.' (June 16) On Kugelmann's advice, and taking account of Engels' suggestions, Marx writes an expository chapter on the form of value which he proposes to include as an appendix. In sending proofs to Engels, he writes: 'I hope you will be satisfied with these 4 sheets. Your satisfaction is more important to me than anything the rest of the world might say. Whatever happens, the bourgeoisie will remember my carbuncles as long as it lives.' (June 22) Exchange of views with Engels on the origin of surplus value and the transformation of value into price of production. The resolution of certain problems presupposes analyses and developments reserved for Books II and III of *Capital*. 'If I dealt in advance with all the objections I should completely spoil the dialectical method of development.' (to Engels, June 27) Marx writes the Preface to *Capital* (July 25), in which he formulates the central thesis of his work: 'Even if a society has discovered the natural law which governs the movement — and it is the ultimate aim of my book to reveal the economic law of motion of modern society — it can neither leap over the natural phases of development nor legislate them out of existence. But it can shorten and moderate the birth pangs.'

August–December: Marx speaks at a meeting of the general Council on the subject of an official participation of IWMA representatives in the Congress of the League of Peace and Freedom, convened for September 9 in Geneva. He declares that the Congress of the Workers' International was 'in itself a peace congress, as the union of the working classes of the different countries must ultimately make international wars impossible.' As for standing armies, which had emerged mainly after the revolution of 1848, they are the inevitable result of the present social situation, and serve chiefly to repress the working class. The partisans of peace at any price want to leave Russia alone in possession of the means for carrying on a war against Europe. 'But the very existence of such a power as Russia was enough for all the other countries to keep their armies intact.' (August 13) On sending the final proofs to the publisher, Marx writes to his friend: 'It is thanks to you that I have been able to do all that! Without your sacrifices for me, I should never have been able to accomplish the immense work for the three books. With my heart full of gratitude, I embrace you.' (August 16) Marx works on Book II of *Capital*. *Capital* Book I appears at the beginning of September, in an edition of 1000 copies. Marx is informed by his friends Eccarius and Lessner, delegates of the general Council, of the developments at the second International Congress at Lausanne. (September 5-9) With regard to the Geneva Peace Congress: 'Naturally, it is the Russians who have fabricated the Geneva Peace Congress and have sent their *well worn out* agent Bakunin to do it.' (to Engels, October 4) In November and December Engels publishes four reviews of *Capital* in German journals. Liebknecht, who was elected to the North German Reichstag on August 31, makes his first speech (in the debate on the passport law). (September 30) Marx studies the Irish question and concludes that the separation of Ireland and England is inevitable. He recognises proletarian and socialist tendencies among the Fenians and formulates possible objectives of their struggle: autonomous government; an agrarian revolution; protectionist tariffs against England. He speaks frequently in the meetings of the Central Council on the question of Ireland. Joseph Dietzgen, a German artisan tanner living in St Petersburg, pays tribute to Marx 'for the inestimable merit he has earned through his researches, both for science and for the working class.' He finds in the *Critique of Political Economy* a profound philosophy, the outline of which he sketches. Marx sends Dietzgen's letter (of October 24) to Kugelmann, and quotes Engels, who 'rightly remarks that self-taught philosophy — produced by workers themselves — had made great progress in the work of this tanner by comparison with the cobbler, Jacob Böhme, and that no-one other than "German" workers is capable of such intellectual achievements.' Marx gets in touch with Elie Reclus about a French translation of *Capital*, for which he envisages making a number of modifications in various sections, while reserving for himself the right to make a 'final revision of the French text.' (to V Schily, November 30) For the benefit of ladies and other uninformed readers: 'Will you show your wife the following sections, which I believe a beginner could read: the working day, co-operation, the division of labour and machinery, and finally, primitive accumulation.' (to Kugelmann, November 30) A talk on Ireland to the Association of German Workers. (December 16)

1868

Annual Report to the Brussels Congress
Gladstone and the Russian Loan
Resolution on the International Alliance of Socialist Democracy

January-May: Suffering from carbuncles and lack of money, Marx lives in effect on subsidies from Engels. He works on Book III of *Capital* (ground rent; agricultural chemistry). He appears fairly satisfied with a review of his book by E Dühring although the author has not understood what is new in it. (to Engels, January 8) Schweitzer publishes a series of articles on *Capital* in the *Social-Demokrat*. At the suggestion of W Liebknecht, Engels thinks of publishing a pamphlet entitled 'Marx and Lassalle'. He continues to write anonymous articles on *Capital* for German papers. Marx to Engels: 'All things considered, there will be no war this year. They are too afraid of the workers at home. But the Russians won't miss any chance of provocation. They will be done for if they don't succeed in plunging Germany and France into war.' In a letter to Kugelmann about E Dühring, the critic of Marx and Hegel: 'He knows very well that my method of analysis is not Hegelian, because I am a materialist, while Hegel is an idealist. Hegel's dialectic is the fundamental form of all dialectic; but not until it has cast off its mystical form, and that is precisely what characterises my method.' (March 6) The carbuncles prevent Marx from working. He decides to have arsenic treatment. Marriage of Laura Marx to Paul Lafargue. (April 2) Freiligrath thanks Marx for sending him *Capital*, a work with which the author has erected for himself a *monumentum aere perennis*. 'I know that young merchants and industrialists on the Rhine are very enthusiastic about the book.' (April 3) Marx writes to his daughter Laura, asking her to make enquiries about the fate of the copies of *Capital* which have been sent to Schily for Jaclard, Taine and Reclus: 'You'll certainly fancy, my dear child, that I am very fond of books, because I trouble you with them at so unseasonable a time. But you would be quite mistaken. I am a machine condemned to devour them, and then throw them in a changed form on the dunghill of history.' (April 11) Exchange of views with Engels on the problems of Book III of *Capital* (rate of profit and rate of surplus value). Marx sends Engels a detailed plan of the process of circulation of capital. (April 30) At Marx's suggestion, the general Council of the International decides to denounce the Belgian government which is responsible for the massacre of striking miners at Charleroi (May 4). Marx to Joseph Dietzgen:

'When I have got rid of the burden of economics I shall write a work on the dialectic. The real laws of dialectic are already contained in Hegel, but in a mystical form. It is a matter of stripping away this form.' (May 9)

June–December: Visit to Manchester accompanied by Eleanor. Contrary to an earlier resolution, Marx suggests to the General Council that the next Congress of the International be held in Brussels. Jenny and Eleanor are ill with scarlet fever. Following a campaign conducted by Felix Pyat in Paris and London in the name of the French section of the IWMA, advocating the assassination of Napoleon III, Marx gets the General Council to adopt a resolution which repudiates and condemns the actions of the French publicist. On an anonymous review accusing Marx of having plagiarised F Bastiat in his theory of value: 'The poor fellow does not see that, even if there were no chapter on "value" in my book, the analysis I make of real conditions would contain the proof and demonstration of the real value relation.' (to Kugelmann, July 11) Marx declines an invitation from W Liebknecht (who had just attempted a rapprochement with Schweitzer) to attend the next Congress of workers' associations in Nürnberg: 'For my part, as a member of the General Council, I must adopt a neutral attitude with regard to the various organised workers' groups.' (to Engels, July 29) Marx intervenes in the debates of the General Council on the agenda of the Brussels Congress. His draft resolution on the effects of mechanisation is adopted. (July 28) Marx is invited to take part in the forthcoming conference of the General Association of German Workers but is unable to accept as he is occupied with the preparation for the IWMA Congress. In his reply, he congratulates the conference for putting in its programme declarations of aims which should be those of all workers' movements: 'The struggle for complete political freedom, regulation of the working day, and systematic international cooperation of the working class in the great historical task which it has to accomplish for the whole of society.' (*Social-Demokrat* August 28) Marx draws up the General Council's report to the Brussels Congress, which concludes: 'Nothing but an international bond of the working classes can ever ensure their definitive triumph. This want has given birth to the International Working Men's Association. That association has not been hatched by a sect or a theory. It is the spontaneous growth of the proletarian movement, which itself is the offspring of the natural and irrepressible tendencies of modern society. Profoundly convinced of the greatness of its mission, the IWMA will allow itself neither to be intimidated nor misled. Its destiny henceforward coalesces with the historical progress of the class that bears in its hands the regeneration of mankind.' (published in the *Times*, September 9) Marx is re-elected to the General Council as corresponding secretary for Germany. (September 19) The police dissolve the General Association of German Workers. Marx instructs W Liebknecht on the tactics to employ in his conflict with Schweitzer. He is informed by N F Danielson, a Russian economist and socialist (Narodnik) that a Petersburg publisher wants to produce a Russian translation of *Capital*. Marx tells Kugelmann about it: 'By an irony of fate the Russians, whom I have combatted unceasingly for 25 years, in German as well as in French and English, have always been my "protectors". In Paris, in 1843–44, the Russian aristocrats looked after me. My book against Proudhon (1847) as well as the *Critique* (1859) found more readers in Russia than anywhere else. And the first foreign country to translate *Capital* is Russia.' (to Kugelmann, October 12) Urged by Schweitzer, to intervene in his conflict with Liebknecht, Marx sets out his views and criticisms of Lassalle's policy, and of the sectarian and religious character of his activity: 'He fell into the same error as Proudhon; not seeking a real basis for his agitation in the real elements of the class movement, but wanting to direct its course according to a doctrinaire recipe.' He criticises the draft statutes drawn up by Schweitzer for the trade unions: a sectarian draft, inapplicable in Germany, where the worker is brought up to respect authority and hierarchy. What the worker in Germany must be taught is how to 'walk by himself.' (October 13) The French members of the IWMA come under the influence of Pyat. The General Council authorises Marx to repudiate the French branch should the occasion arise. Marx studies the problems of ground rent and gives particular attention to the rural commune and its role in the various economic systems among the Slavs, especially in Russia. L Büchner sends Marx his *Six Lectures on the Darwinian Theory*. Engels tells Marx of his decision to settle all his debts and assure him an annual income of £350 for 5 or 6 years at least (November 29). Exchange of views with Engels on the works of the historian E Tériot who makes some revelations concerning Louis Bonaparte's *coup d'état*. To Kugelmann (December 5): 'Is your wife also active in the great German campaign for women's emancipation? I think that German women are beginning in this way to drive their menfolk toward self-emancipation.' On Marx's proposal, the General Council rejects the request by the Bakunist Alliance for admission to the IWMA as an independent organisation. From Geneva, Bakunin writes to Marx renewing his assurance of friendship and acknowledging

the correctness of Marx's views on the economic revolution: 'At the
moment I am doing what you began to do more than 20 years ago ...
My country now is the International, of which you are one of the
principal founders. You see therefore, my dear friend, that I am your
disciple, and proud of it.' (December 22)

1869

The 18th Brumaire of Louis Bonaparte, 2nd edn.
Report to the Fourth Congress of the IWMA
Appeals, decisions, manifestos, resolutions
Address to the National Labour Union of the United States — Resolu-
tion of the GC on the attitude of the British Government on the
question of amnesty for the incarcerated Fenians.

January–March: 'I have been a grandfather since January 1st. I received
a little boy as a Christmas present.' (to Kugelmann, February 11) Marx
gives the General Council information on the strikes of the Rouen
cotton workers and proposes sending help to the strikers. (January 5)
Engels tells Marx of the death of Ernest Jones: 'Another one of the old
generation has gone.' (January 26) At a meeting of the General Council
Marx proposes that the trade unions be urged to come to the aid of the
striking weavers and dyers of Basle. (February 2) Brief visit to Manchester. In a letter to Kugelmann, Marx draws attention to the
conspiracy of silence of the 'expert mandarins' and the bourgeois
reactionary press against *Capital*. He tells him of a letter sent by Arnold
Ruge to a Manchester merchant; this is what Ruge says about *Capital*:
'It is an epoch-making work. It throws a brilliant, sometimes blinding,
light upon the development, the decline, the birth pangs and the times
of terrible suffering in different social periods.' (February 11) Marx
resumes his scientific work and studies the literature on banks and
credit. On his proposal, the General Council decides to put on the
agenda of the next Congress of the IWMA the problems of landed
property, credit, and general education. Lafargue informs Marx that
Blanqui possesses a copy of the anti-Proudhon *Poverty of Philosophy*
which he lends to all his friends. 'Blanqui has the highest regard for you
... He has found the most delightful term I have heard for Proudhon;
he calls him a hygrometer.' (Marx to Engels, March 1) Marx tells
Kugelmann about some recent historical publications in French (Tériot,

Castille, Vermorel, Tridon): 'The Parisians are studying their revolutionary past, to prepare themselves for the new revolutionary outbreak which is imminent.' (March 3) In response to a request from the Alliance of Socialist Democracy the General Council decides, at Marx's instigation, to accept the sections of the dissolved Alliance in the IWMA, on condition that their programme conforms with the principles laid down in the statutes of the IWMA. Marx draws up the reply which is to go to the Alliance, and referring to one of the articles of the programme, he writes: 'It is not the logically impossible *equalisation of classes*, but the historically necessary, superseding "abolition of classes" . . . this true secret of the proletarian movement, which forms the great aim of the IWMA.' (Circular of March 9) From a letter to Engels: 'I intend to become a naturalised Englishman, so as to be able to go to Paris in complete safety. Unless I make this journey there will never be a French edition of my book.' (March 20)

April–July: Marx gives a report to the General Council on the activity of the Social Democrats in the North German Reichstag, where Bebel spoke in favour of the IWMA. (April 13) Lafargue sends Marx his French translation of the *Communist Manifesto*. Marx to Engels: 'There is no hurry about that. I don't want Lafargue to burn his fingers prematurely.' He sends to Engels Diderot's *Rameau's Nephew*, 'this unique masterpiece,' and quotes passages from a commentary by Hegel. (April 15) The General Council approves an appeal drawn up by Marx to the workers of Europe and the US to come to the aid of the striking Belgian miners who are victims of the massacres ordered by their Government. (May 4) Marx writes an address to the Union of American Workers urging them to oppose the war which the leaders of the Republican party are preparing against Great Britain: 'On you . . . depends the glorious task to prove to the world that now at last the working classes are bestriding the scene of history no longer as servile retainers, but as independent actors, conscious of their own responsibility and able to command peace where their would-be masters shout war.' (May 12) Together with Eleanor, Marx goes to stay with Engels in Manchester for three weeks. He visits the English geologist J R Dakyns whom he describes in a letter to his daughter Jenny. Speaking of the Positivists: 'We agree that the only positive thing about them is their arrogance.' (June 10) He writes the preface to the second edition of *The Eighteenth Brumaire* and criticises the 'Caesarism' (a term then in vogue), naiveté and superficiality of the lovers of historical analogies: 'Sismondi's important remark is forgotten: the Roman proletariat lived at the expense of society, while modern society lives at the expense of the proletariat. Given the enormous difference between the material and economic conditions of the class struggles in the ancient world and the struggles of modern classes, their political animators have as little resemblance as the Archbishop of Canterbury and the high priest Solomon.' (June 23) Engels leaves the firm 'Ermen & Engels'. 'Hurrah! Today I have finished with *le doux commerce*, and am a free man!' (to Marx, July 1) Marx: 'My heartiest congratulations on your flight from Egyptian captivity!' (to Engels, July 3) Marx declines Liebknecht's invitation to take part in the Congress of Workers' Associations at Eisenach. He insists on the necessity for the new organisation to free itself from any kind of sectarianism (Lassallean) to turn itself into an independent party; the transformation ought to be seen as 'the free action of the workers themselves.' (to Engels, July 3) In a discussion in the General Council on the question of landed property, which had been placed on the agenda of the next Congress of the IWMA, Marx criticises the point of view put forward by the Proudhonists at the Brussels Congress, and presents the change to collective ownership of mines, forests and land in general as a social and economic necessity. (July 6) Visit to Paul and Laura Lafargue in Paris, under the name of Williams (July 7-12). Marx gives Engels an account of the visit and draws his attention to a remarkable speech by Raspail (July 14). Marx speaks to the General Council on the question of the right of inheritance which had been raised at the Geneva Congress by the followers of Bakunin. 'First the means for a transformed state of things must be got, then the right (to inheritance) would disappear of itself.' (July 20)

August-December: Engels publishes his first biographical articles on Marx and says of *Capital*: 'This work contains the fruits of a whole lifetime's study. It is the political economy of the working class expressed in a scientific form.' (*Die Zukunft* August 11) The General Council adopts a resolution drawn up by Marx on the question of the right of inheritance. 'Like all other civil legislation, the laws of inheritance are not the *cause* but the *effect*, the juridical *consequences* of the *existing economic organisation* of society, based upon private property in the means of production ...' Among the transitional measures to be taken while awaiting the establishment of common ownership, the resolution recommends increasing the inheritance taxes and restricting the right of inheritance. (August 3) Liebknecht informs Marx of the foundation at Eisenach of the Social-Democratic Labour Party and of the decision by the Congress to affiliate with the IWMA. At two meetings of the General Council, Marx speaks on the problem of public education in modern society. He declares himself in favour of a national system of education which ought not, however, to be controlled by government. Fees should be paid only for higher education. 'Neither in the elementary schools nor in higher education should one teach subjects which could have a party or class interpretation.' (August 10 and 17) Marx writes the Annual Report of the General Council of the IWMA for the Congress in Basle. (September 6-11) Marx, accompanied by his daughter Jenny, goes to stay with Dr Kugelmann in Hanover. On the way they visit Joseph Dietzgen's home in Siegburg. In Hanover, Marx receives a delegation of Lassallean trade unionists to whom he explains his views on the role of trade unions as a 'school of socialism'; the unions, far from having to associate themselves with political organisations, can themselves act as 'the real workers' party and form a bulwark against the power of capital.' (September 30) In a letter to Engels, Marx criticises W Liebknecht's indecisive position on the question of nationalisation of land as it is posed in Germany: he alludes to the 'style of 1789,' now anachronistic (October 30). He returns to the study of the Irish question. In the General Council, he emphasises the importance of the national emancipation of Ireland for the social emancipation of the English proletariat. (October–November) Having received from Danielson the book by N Flerovski on *The Situation of the Working Class in Russia* (1869) Marx begins to study Russian. Another attack of boils. He helps with the translation of an address of the Land and Labour League (founded in October) whose programme envisages the nationalisation of the land; free, secular, and compulsory general education; the abolition of standing armies, etc. In several meetings, Marx comments on the policy of the British government toward the incarcerated Irishmen (Fenians) and denounces Gladstone's duplicity in the matter of an amnesty for the Irish revolutionaries. A resolution on the Fenians, proposed by Marx, is passed unanimously. (November) Discussion with Engels on the theory of ground rent (Carey, Ricardo). (November 19 and 26) Marx writes to Kugelmann outlining his views on the Irish question, a touchstone for the workers' movement in England. (November 29) He returns to the problem in a letter to Engels: 'The English working class will achieve nothing until it is rid of Ireland. The lever must be applied in Ireland.' (December 10) Growing influence of Bakunin in the IWMA. 'He professes to be the guardian of the true proletarian spirit . . . As soon as a Russian infiltrates, all hell breaks loose.' (to Engels, December 7)

1870

Circular and confidential communication concerning Bakunin's activities
Declarations and resolutions of the General Council of the IWMA
For an amnesty for the Fenians
Address of the General Council of the IWMA on the Franco-Prussian War
Second Address of the General Council of the IWMA on the Franco-Prussian War

January-March: In the name of the General Council, Marx draws up a circular addressed to the Federal Council of the IWMA in French Switzerland, which is designed to refute the accusations of Bakunin's followers against the General Council. He emphasises the role of the General Council which, because of its influence on the trade union movement, has control of the 'lever of proletarian revolution' in England, 'the capitalist metropolis.' He defines the IWMA's position on the Irish question ('the nation that brings another into subjection forges its own chains'); the importance of the political struggle as a vehicle of the social movement, etc. (about January 1) Engels is alarmed by Jenny Marx's account of her husband's chronic relapses and lack of care for his health and urges him to change his way of life, if only in order to finish Book II of *Capital*. (January 19) On Flerovski, whom he is reading in Russian and whose originality he admires, Marx writes: 'At all events, it is the most important book that has appeared since your work on *The Condition of the Working Class*.' (February 10) 'His book shows irrefutably that the present situation in Russia in untenable, that the emancipation of the serfs can only accelerate the process of dissolution and that a terrible social revolution is imminent.' (February 12) He writes to Kugelmann about his Russian readings: 'The misery of the Russian peasantry has the same cause as the misery of the French peasantry under Louis XIV: taxes to the State and the *obrok* paid to the great landowers; far from creating poverty, common ownership has, on the contrary, diminished it.' (February 17) With Marx's assistance, his daughter Jenny writes a series of articles on the Irish question advocating an amnesty for the Fenian prisoners. The articles appear under the signature 'J Williams' in *La Marseillaise*. (March-April) Marx works on Book II of *Capital*. The 'positivist proletarians' of Paris having constituted themselves a branch of the IWMA, the General Council, on Marx's proposal, decide to admit them simply as 'proletarians'; 'given that the Comtian principles are contrary to our statutes.' (to Engels, March 19) A group of Russians in Geneva asks Marx to represent them in the

General Council. He agrees and writes to Engels: 'An odd position for me — to function as a representative of young Russia ... In my official reply I praise Flerovski and emphasise that the principal task of the Russian branch is to work for Poland (that is to say, to rid Europe of Russia as a neighbour).' (March 24) In his capacity as secretary of the IWMA for Germany, Marx sends through Kugelmann a 'confidential communication' to the Committee of the German Social-Democratic Party in which he traces Bakunin's attitude and activities from their meeting in London in November 1864 until the creation of the Alliance of Socialist Democracy. He denounces Bakunin's Russian anarchist taste for conspiracies and accuses him of wishing to transform the International into an instrument of his personal ambitions. Marx includes in this document the General Council's circular of January 16. (March 28)

April–July: Marx continues his studies on Ireland. He sets out his views in a letter to S Meyer and A Vogt, German workers who had emigrated to the US and are members of the IWMA, urging them to fight for Irish independence. 'A coalition of German workers with Irish workers (and of course with the English and American workers who accept this idea): that is the enormous task you can now put in hand, in the name of the International.' (April 9) Marx informs Lafargue of the activities of Bakunin whose programme he criticises (abolition of the right of inheritance, equalisation of classes, abstention from all political activity). 'Thus this damned Muscovite has been able to call forth a great public scandal within our ranks, to make his personality a watchword, to infect our Workingmen's Association with the poison of sectarianism, and to paralyse our action through secret intrigue.' (April 19) Marx receives six copies of the first Russian edition of the *Communist Manifesto*, printed at the end of 1869 in Geneva. Bakunin, author(?) of the translation, is not named there. Marx visits the dying Karl Schapper, who recalls his past as a revolutionary militant before 1851, 'Tell all our friends that I have remained faithful to my principles. I am not a theorist. During the period of reaction, I had great difficulty in supporting my family. I have lived as a hard-working man and I die a proletarian.' (Marx to Engels, April 28) The General Council adopts a proclamation drawn up by Marx denouncing the police persecutions in France of which members of the IWMA are victims. 'If the working classes who form the great bulk of all nations, (who produce all their wealth, and in the name of whom even the *usurping* powers pretend to rule) conspire, they conspire publicly as the sun conspires against the darkness, in the full consciousness that without their pale there exists no legitimate power.' (May 3) In a letter to Engels Marx comments, from a legal point of view, on the rumours spread by the English and French press on the possible extradition of Gustave Florens who had been accused of plotting the assassination of Napoleon III. 'If this plot is not a pure invention by the police, at all events it is the greatest stupidity imaginable. Fortunately, the empire can no longer be saved even by the idiocy of its enemies.' (May 7) Marx receives a birthday present from Kugelmann: two pieces of tapestry from Leibniz's study. 'I have hung them in my study. You know my admiration for Leibniz.' (to Engels, May 10) On the subject of the arrests of some of the members of the French section of the IWMA, before and after the May plebiscite: 'the French government has at last done what we wanted for a long time. It has made the political question of empire or republic a matter of life or death for the working class.' (to Engels, May 18) Visit to Manchester with Eleanor (May 23 to June 23). Marx and Engels send directives to the Committee of the German workers' party in relation to the next Congress of the IWMA which is to be held in Mainz. (July 14) The sections in French Switzerland secede. Marx has a resolution passed supporting the Federal Committee against the committee formed by Bakunin and his followers. (June 28) Visit by Hermann Lopatin, a Russian revolutionary, who informs Marx of the fate of N G Chernyshevsky (exiled in Siberia) and of the activity of Nechayev, 'one of the few agents of Bakunin in Russia' who had murdered one of his own supporters. (to Engels, July 5) After the announcement of the French declaration of war on Prussia, Marx is disappointed by manifestations of patriotism in French republican circles and urges the defeat of France: 'The French need a rebuke. If the Prussians are victorious, the centralisation of state power will help the centralisation of the German working class.' The preponderance of the German working class movement over that of France 'will mean at the same time the predominance of our theory over that of Proudhon.' (to Engels, July 20) This preoccupation, and this biassed view, while not appearing in the first address Marx drafts, at the request of the General Council on his Franco–Prussian war, is nevertheless revealed in a passing allusion: 'on Germany's side it is a defensive war:' in other words, in the view of Marx and Engels Germany is fighting for its national existence. The 'dark figure of Russia' is not forgotten in this address. (July 26) Marx writes to Paul and Laura Lafargue, to whom he expresses his disgust with the patriotic demonstrations in both camps: 'Still, there is this consolation, that the workmen protest in Germany as in France. In point of fact, the war of classes is too far developed in both countries to allow any political war whatever to roll back the wheel of history . . . For my own part I should like that both Prussians and French thrashed each other alternately, and that — as I believe will be the case — the Germans got *ultimately* the better of it. I wish this because the defeat of Bonaparte is likely to provoke a revolution in France, while the definite defeat of the Germans would only protract the present state of things for twenty years.' (July 28)

August-December: The General Council adopts Marx's proposal to postpone the Congress of the IWMA because of the war. (August 2) Marx learns through Lopatin that Bakunin is giving it out that he (Marx) is an agent of Bismarck. The same rumour is being spread by certain members of the French branch. (to Engels, August 3) The Marx family stay in Ramsgate for several weeks (August 9-31) Engels and Marx exchange views on the tactics adopted by Liebknecht and Bracke, whose systematic opposition to Bismarck seems to them to be a mistake, given Germany's stake in the war; namely its national existence. 'First, as in 1866 Bismarck is still performing part of our work; in his own way and without wishing it, but he is doing it all the same.' (Engels to Marx, August 15) After reaching agreement with Engels, Marx sends an official letter to the committee of the German Social Democratic Party, urging it to oppose strongly the annexation of Alsace-Lorraine, which will inevitably lead to another war, in which France will have Russia as an ally. On the other hand, if Prussia concludes an honourable peace with France, the inevitable war between Germany and Prussia will 'rid Europe of the Muscovite dictatorship, integrate Prussia into the German nation, permit the Western continent a peaceful development, and finally aid the genesis of the Russian social revolution. . .' (September 5) It is in this spirit that Marx drafts his second address on the war, in which he hails the coming of the Republic in France, and predicts that, should Germany annex any French territory, she will face a racial war against the allied Slav and Latin races; he urges the French workers to 'perform their duty as citizens' and 'not to recapitulate the past, but to build up the future. Let them calmly and resolutely improve the opportunities of Republican liberty, for the work of their own class organisation.' (September 9) During the rest of the year Marx is very active in London workers' circles and in the various sections of the IWMA, with the object of obtaining recognition of the French Republic by the English government. Engels comes to live in London and

establishes himself in a house close to the Marx family. He is elected
a member of the General Council. (October 4) In the November and
December meetings of the General Council Marx makes regular reports
on the development of the International in Europe and the USA. To
Kugelmann: 'Whatever the outcome of the war, it has taught the proletariat to handle arms, and that is the best guarantee for the future.'
(December 15) Marx frequently meets the Russian revolutionary,
J L Tomanovskaya, who informs him about the activities of the Russian
section of the IWMA in Geneva, and discusses with him the prospects
for the rural commune in Russia. From Petersburg Lopatin tells Marx
of his plan to arrange the escape of Nicolai G Chernyshevsky.

1871

Address on the Civil War in France
Resolutions of the Conference of Delegates of the IWMA
General Rules and Administrative Regulations of the IWMA
Declarations, denials, talks, tracts, interviews, appeals

January-April: Marx transmits to Lafargue, who has settled in Bor-
deaux, information received in confidence from Germany which was
intended for the Government of National Defence, concerning the
difficulties of the Prussian army in France. In an open letter to the
Daily News, he attacks Bismarck, who has had Liebknecht and Bebel
imprisoned on a charge of high treason. Marx concludes 'France —
and her cause is fortunately far from desperate — fights at this moment
not only for her own independence, but for the liberty of Germany
and Europe.' (January 19) In the General Council there is a clash
between Marx and Odger, a trade unionist who, in opposition to the
second address on the war, had publicly praised the French government. In his letters to Lafargue and Kugelmann Marx violently attacks
'Jules Favre & Co', who by signing the armistice have made Bismarck
the supreme power in France. (February 4) In a dicussion of the
attitude of the English working class to the Franco–Prussian war, Marx
criticises both the Gladstone government, which has delayed recognising the French Republic, and the inadequate action of the English
workers. In his interventions in the General Council he frequently takes
up this question and attacks England's Russophile policy. When news of
the Paris Commune is received, Marx persuades the Council to approve

a campaign of demonstrations of sympathy. Marx is given information by A Serraillier, a member of the General Council, about the events in Paris and the measures taken by the Commune. Léo Frankel, a delegate to the Commune's Commission for Labour and Commerce, writes to Marx to ask for his advice 'on the social reforms to be undertaken', for 'if we could bring about a radical change in social relations, the revolution of March 18 would be the most fruitful of all the revolutions that history has recorded up to the present time.' (March 30)

April–July: In a letter to Liebknecht, Marx makes some criticisms of the Commune: 'It seems that if the Parisians succumb it will be their own fault, but this fault is due to too much honesty. The Central Committee has allowed Thiers time to centralise his forces, by hesitating to start a civil war and losing precious time in organising the Commune, instead of marching on Versailles immediately.' (April 6) A few months later he takes up the subject again in two letters to Kugelmann and eulogises 'our heroic party comrades in Paris' who, as he had predicted in the *Eighteenth Brumaire* (1852), have tried to break the state bureaucratic and military machine, instead of seizing it in order to make it serve their own ends. It is this destruction of the state power which constitutes the 'precondition of any genuine revolution on the continent'. (April 12) Reprimanding Kugelmann for having compared the Commune with the events of June 1849, Marx emphasises the importance of 'chance' in history and declares that 'through the struggle in Paris, the battle of the working class against the capitalist class and its state has entered a new phase'; 'whatever the immediate result, a new starting-point of historic and universal significance has been gained.' (April 17) These themes are further developed by Marx in the *Address on the Civil War in France*, on which he works until the end of May, with interruptions due to illness. A document made public by the republican government reveals that Karl Vogt, the slanderer of Marx in 1859-60, has been paid from the secret funds of Napoleon III.

May–July: Marx meets delegates of the Commune and, through them, transmits information to L Frankel and E Varlin, telling them of the secret agreements reached between Bismarck and Favre. 'I have sent several hundred letters in your cause, to all corners of the world where we have branches. The working class in any case was in favour of the Commune from the beginning.' (May 18) On May 30 Marx reads his *Address on the Civil War in France* to the General Council. In the first

draft of this address he writes that the Commune revolution was
directed not against the *form* of the state power 'but against the *State*
itself, this supernationalist abortion of society,' and that it was 'a
resumption, by the people, for the people, of its own social life.' The
Address is adopted without discussion and is published as a pamphlet.
For several months Marx continues to collect material on the events in
France and the activities of the Commune. At the same time, he
devotes himself to the organisation of help for the refugees of the
Commune. In a declaration sent to the press he attacks J Favre's
circular, the aim of which is to have members of the IWMA hunted
down by all the governments of Europe. (June 13) On the subject of
the next part of *Capital*, Marx tells Danielson that he thinks 'a complete
recasting of the manuscript' is necessary. (June 13) Marx is criticised
in the General Council by the Englishmen Odger and Lucraft, because
of certain passages in his *Address* relating to the Versailles government,
and in reply to the attacks which had appeared in the London press,
Marx lets it be known that he is the author of the *Address*. (June 26)
Marx grants an interview to the London correspondent of the New
York *World*, published on July 18, in which he gives details of the
relations between certain people in positions of responsibility in the
Commune and the IWMA, but denies that the rising in Paris is the work
of the International. He explains the nature and the objectives of the
IWMA, whose principal aim is to give material and moral support to the
spontaneous and autonomous movements of the workers of the world.
Marx writes an address to the Central Committee of the American
sections of the IWMA, denouncing the hypocritical attitude of the
American ambassador in Paris, E B Washbourne, during the civil war
and the Commune. (July 11) On Engels' proposal, the General Council
decides to organise an international Conference of the IWMA in
September. (July 25)

August–December: Marx sends to A Hubert, a communard who had
emigrated to London, and who is also a member of the IWMA, particulars and documents to be included in the defence dossier of the
Communards in the coming trail. (August 10) Visit to Brighton for a
ten-day rest (August 17–26) Marx and Engels devote themselves to
preparing for the IWMA Conference, which is to be held from September 17–22. Marx makes long speeches at all the meetings in order to
explain and move the resolutions prepared by the General Council. He
defines the objectives of the Conference: to reorganise the IWMA in
order to respond to the needs of the situation; to counter attempts by

governments to destroy the Association; to settle the conflict with the Swiss dissidents. He analyses the structure of the trade unions, 'an aristocratic minority', which do not welcome poor workers; they will only be able to attain revolutionary goals by carrying on political activity with the help of the International. Political action by the working class is necessary, for it has every interest in being represented in parliaments, so as to be heard throughout the world: 'to get workers into the parliaments is equivalent to a victory over the governments; but suitable men must be chosen, not people like Tolain'; reaction is permanent and universal, even in the United States and in England, although it takes another form there. 'We must say to governments: we know that you are the armed power directed against the proletarians, and we will fight you with peaceful means where possible and with arms where necessary.' Secret groupings within the IWMA must be prohibited, even in countries where the right of association does not exist: 'This type of organisation is inconsistent with the development of the proletarian movement, for instead of educating the workers, these societies subject them to authoritarian and mysterious laws which shackle their independence and turn their consciousness in a false direction.' In a talk given on the occasion of the IWMA's seventh anniversary, Marx compares the International with the early Christians: 'The persecutions in Rome could not save the Empire; similarly, the persecutions of the International at the present time will not save the existing order. What is new in the International is that it was created by the workers themselves for the workers.' The Commune, the most important workers' movement so far, represents the conquest of political power by the working class; this conquest is necessary in order to abolish class domination, following a period of the dictatorship of the proletariat. 'The task of the International is to organise and unite the forces of the workers for the future struggle.' (September 25) Marx is re-elected corresponding secretary for Russia. (October 3) He prepares the definitive text of the resolutions for the London Conference. Marx becomes ill from overwork; he cannot attend the meetings of the General Council during the whole of November. In a letter to F Bolte, a member of the New York Federal Council of the IWMA, he sets out his ideas on the genesis and the tasks of the International, which he compares with the historical movement of the socialist sects; in addition he emphasises the importance of the political movement of the working class (for example, the winning of the Eight Hour Law) as distinct from the economic movement (local strikes etc.). (November 23)

1872

January–May: Marx prepares the second edition of *Capital*. He takes part in the debates of the General Council, which concern the relations with the English Federal Council, and calls for a change in the statutes. Through the mediation of Charles Longuet, he makes contact with Joseph Roy for a French translation of *Capital*; also with the publisher Maurice Lachatre, with whom he concludes a contract, at the beginning of February, for the publication of his book in instalments at the author's expense. He asks his cousin August Philips for financial help, but the latter refuses: 'In case of need, I should be willing to help a friend or relation with money, but I shall not do so for your political and revolutionary purposes.' (January 26) In response to decisions taken in November 1871 at Sonvilliers, by the Congress of the dissidents from the International who are concentrated in the Jura Federation, Marx and Engels draft a confidential circular in French to which they give the title *Alleged Divisions in the International*. This 40-page pamphlet gives a history of the contentions between the General Council and Bakunin and his partisans, since the circular of December 1868 on the Alliance of Socialist Democracy. Marx works on the revision of *Capital* for the second German edition and goes over the French translation submitted to him by Joseph Roy. He gives the General Council a report on the split which has occurred in the North American Federation of the International. He sends the resolutions to F A Sorge, secretary of the provisional Federal Council in New York (March 15). With a view to a demonstration to celebrate the first anniversary of the Commune, Marx draws up three draft resolutions in which 'the glorious movement of March 18' is characterised as 'the dawn of the great social revolution which will set men free for ever from the class system.' At the end of March, the Russian edition of *Capital* is published in a printing of 3,000 copies, of which 900 are sold within six weeks. The Censorship Committee has authorised its publication: 'even though the author, according to his convictions, is a thoroughgoing socialist, and the whole book has a fundamentally and resolutely socialist character; it is a book which is not very accessible to the ordinary reader and its form is "rigorously and mathematically scientific".' (See Marx to Sorge, June 21) Marx informs the General Council of the conclusion of the Leipzig trial of Liebknecht, Bebel and Hepner for high treason. (April 2) At the same meeting he, with two other members, is instructed to draft a protest against the police terror of which the Irish sections of the IWMA are victims. The General Council adopts a declaration proposed by Marx directed against the activities of certain English and foreign groups in London which are trying to usurp the name of the General Council. (May 11) Marx corrects the proofs of the second German edition and the French translation of *Capital*. In the latter he makes important alterations 'in order to make things clearer to the French.' (to Sorge, May 23) He thanks Danielson for the copy of the Russian edition of *Capital*; he finds the translation 'masterly'. He asks Danielson to give him particulars of Bakunin's influence in Russia and his relations with Nechayev, who had been tried in January 1871 for the assassination of the student Ivanov. He announces that he will retire from the General Council after the next Congress of the IWMA so that he can finish *Capital*.

June-August: In his interventions in the General Council, Marx takes up a position against the Belgian, Swiss and English members of the International, who are refusing to apply the 1871 resolutions concerned especially with the political action of the working class and are challenging the authority of the General Council. In the bulletin of the Jura Federation Bakunin describes Marx as a 'metaphysician' who has 'habits of mind which seem to have remained with him from the Hegelian school.' On Marx's proposal, Holland is chosen as the site of the next Congress of the IWMA. (June 11) Marx devotes himself almost entirely to the preparations of the coming Congress of the International: 'The next Congress will begin on the first Monday in September 1872 at The Hague . . . It is a matter of life and death for the International.' (to Sorge, June 21) In their preface to the new edition of the *Communist Manifesto*, Marx and Engels call to mind the experience of the Commune and repeat the lesson set forth in the *Address* of 1871: 'The working class cannot simply take possession of the state machine just as it is and use it for its own ends.' (June 24) Discussion in the Central Council on the Revision of the Statutes of the IWMA. Marx and Engels supports a proposal by Vaillant to insert in the text of the general statutes the resolution of the London Conference on the political action of the working class. Marx also suggests an addition to the Statutes, specifying that the sections must be composed of a minimum of three quarters of wage earners. (July 23) To Kugelmann: 'At the International Congress . . . it will be a matter of life and death for the International, and before I leave it I should like at least to protect it from the disruptive elements. Germany must therefore have the greatest possible number of representatives.' (July 29) The first delivery of the French edition of *Capital* comes from the printers. Marx receives the manuscript of Chernyshevsky's *Letters Without Address* from Danielson and asks him to send immediately a blackmailing letter from Nechayev, which compromises Bakunin, concerning an advance which the latter had obtained from a Russian publisher for translating *Capital*. Marx will refer in this letter to his dealings with Bakunin at the Hague Congress.

September–December: At the Congress Marx reads the General Council's report, in which he recalls the persecutions to which the International has been subjected by the Bonapartist and Prussian governments, and the crusade against the International following Jules Favre's circular to the foreign powers. As for Russia, its government 'has found in the general hounding of the International a pretext for increasing reaction at home.' The report ends with these words: 'Deputies of the working class, you are meeting together to strengthen the fighting organisations of a league whose object is the emancipation of labour and the abolition of national struggles. Almost at the same moment the crowned heads who bear the identity of the old world are meeting in Berlin to forge new chains and prepare new wars. Long live the International Working Men's Association!' (September 3) The Congress adopts a proposal from Marx to strengthen the powers of the General Council. It also adopts (by a small majority, it is true) the proposal from Engels, Marx and other members of the General Council, to transfer the Council's office for 1872–73 to New York. In the commision responsible for reaching a decision on the Alliance, Marx does his utmost to demonstrate, with Russian documents to support him, that they are dealing with a secret society whose principal aim is to exploit the International. (September 6) The resolution of 1871 on the political action of the working class is approved for inclusion in the IWMA statutes. (September 7) At a workers' meeting convened in Amsterdam, Marx speaks of the results of the Hague Congress and comments on the resolution dealing with the necessity for political action and the conquest of power: 'one day the worker must seize political power in order to set up a new organisation of labour; he must overturn the old politics which maintains the old institutions or, like the early Christians, who neglected and despised such action, he will lose the kingdom of heaven on earth.' In countries like America, England, and perhaps also Holland, the workers might be able to attain their ends by peaceful means. But in most of the countries of continental Europe the 'yeast of our revolution must be violence.' In conclusion, Marx declares that he will continue his work in order to lay the foundations of international workers' solidarity. 'No, I am not retiring from the International, and the rest of my life, like all my past endeavours, will be devoted to the triumph of the social ideas which will one day lead – you can be sure of this – to the rule of the proletariat throughout the world.' (September 8) Marx and Engels write the resolutions of the Hague Congress; they carry on a correspondence with F A Sorge, the secretary of the General Council in New York, and inform him of the activity of the federations and sections of the International in Europe. Marriage of Jenny with Charles Longuet. (October 10) Marx is absorbed in checking the French translation of *Capital* and gets Longuet to help him with it. Engels to Sorge: 'Lafargue and Longuet are both in London and so Father Marx is surrounded by his whole family.' (December 7) Conflict with John Hales who is conducting a campaign against Marx in the English Federal Council, following Marx's statement at the Hague Congress on the corruption of the leaders of the British workers. Danielson informs Marx of Lopatin's fate – exile in Siberia after his vain attempt to help Chernyshevsky escape. In his reply, Marx asks Danielson for details with a view to a publication on the life and personality of Chernyshevsky 'so as to arouse sympathy for him in the West.' (December 12) The minority in the British Federal Council meets at Marx's house to draw up a manifesto against the secessionists. The document defending the Hague resolutions is published as a pamphlet. (December 31)

1873

Capital 2nd German edition
Political Neutrality
Postscript to the Second edition of *Capital*
The Alliance of Socialist Democracy and the IWMA

Some biographers have said, with some exaggeration perhaps, that the last ten years of Marx's life were like a slow agony; certainly, long periods of poverty as well as physical and mental distress had undermined his health, which deteriorates from this time. He suffers from chronic cephalalgy which, added to the hepatitis contracted in the 50's, will force him, in view of the risk of apoplexy, to restrict his activity and to seek relief in cures and changes of climate. He will try on several occasions to re-write Book II of *Capital* and will contribute, not without difficulty, to Engels' *Anti-Dühring*. The rest of his activity will be limited to correspondence and a few articles. Nevertheless — a most improbable thing in this final stage which was so unfruitful in original writing — Marx will fill about 50 notebooks, almost exclusively devoted to extracts from his reading: nearly 3,000 pages of microscopic writing. The passion for reading, which we have seen in the Marx of the great creative periods, will turn during the remainder of his life into a mania for note-taking; and we disregard here the 'tons' of statistical material which will leave Engels dumbfounded. The friend to whom Marx and his family owe the peace of these last years will show even more fully his affection and comradeship. In numerous writings, he will defend Marx's theory and vigorously diffuse their common political ideas.

January-May: Marx sends to Enrico Bignami (on the staff of the journal *La Plèbe*) an article entitled 'L'indifferenza in materia politica' ('Political Neutrality') intended for the *Almanacco republicano*. He attacks the 'doctors of social science', preachers of 'social liquidation' and apostles of the eternal principles of 'liberty, autonomy and anarchy', who despise all political and economic action. Marx defines the two forms of the struggle to be conducted: on the one hand, to gain by legal and peaceful means reforms such as the limitation of the working day, the prohibition of child labour, compulsory primary education, etc., and on the other hand, to struggle, by violent means if necessary, 'to replace the dictatorship of the bourgeoisie by the revolutionary dictatorship' of the workers. Marx drafts one of the last official documents of the International, a circular of the British Federal Council, in which he replies to the attacks of the dissident federal council inspired by John Hales. (*The International Herald*, January 25) He reads the Russian books sent by Danielson, especially works on agricultural conditions and the peasant question since the emancipation of the serfs. In a letter to Bolte, he criticises the General Council in New York for having suspended the Jurassian Federation: 'Everyone and every group has the right to leave the International: when that happens, the General Council ought simply to record this resignation officially, but certainly not suspend those involved.' (February 12) He asks Danielson for information on the controversy in 1856 between the liberal philosopher Chicherin and the Slavophile historian Bieliayev about the historical development of communal property in Russia. 'Every historical analogy speaks against Chicherin. How could it be that in Russia this institution was introduced purely as a fiscal measure, and an appurtenance of serfdom, whereas everywhere else it arises spontaneously, and constitutes a necessary stage in the evolution of free people?' (March 22) Danielson sends Marx a bibliographical note on landed property in Russia. (April 1) Marx suffers from acute cephalalgy and goes to Manchester to consult a doctor friend. He is told to limit his activity to a maximum of four hours' work a day. (May 22–June 3) Engels sends Marx a series of 'dialectical' comments on the natural sciences. He takes as a starting point the concept of body-movement, knowledge of the forms of movement being identical with knowledge of bodies; applied to physical and chemical phenomena this principle would enable one to envisage, in organic chemistry, the artificial manufacture of living material. (May 30) Carl Schorlemmer, professor of chemistry at Manchester and a close friend of Marx and Engels, expresses agreement with the latter's ideas. Marx discusses with Samuel Moore (the future translator of *Capital* into English) the possibility of determining mathematically 'the principal laws of crises' from price movements, discount rates, etc. (to Engels, May 31)

June–December: Publication in Hamburg of the second edition of *Capital*. In his postscript (dated January 24, 1873) Marx writes that the 'understanding which *Capital* quickly found in wide circles of the German working class is the best reward for my labours'. He also cites a Russian reviewer whose exposition of his (Marx's) dialectical method, the 'direct opposite' of Hegel's, he approves: 'The mystification which the dialectic suffered in Hegel's hands does not prevent him from having been the first to expound the general forms of its movement . . . In Hegel the dialectic stands on its head. It must be turned the right way up again in order to discover the rational kernel in the mystical shell.' Marx continues to revise the French translation of his book. In a letter to Bebel, Engels, in the name of Marx and himself, sketches the broad tactical lines to be followed by the German Social Democratic Party in order to influence the working masses who are still indifferent to the political struggle. It is less important to achieve immediate successes by affecting a union with the compromised leaders

of the Lassallean party than to establish 'a single powerful force.' 'As
Hegel said (in the old days) "A party shows itself to be victorious when
it separates and is able to survive the separation".' (June 20) Marx
studies the materials sent by Danielson on agricultural conditions and
communal land ownership in Russia. Marx and Engels write the conclusion of the pamphlet on the *Alliance of Socialist Democracy*, prepared
by Engels and Lafargue on the basis of massive documentation, which
throws light on every aspect of the public or clandestine activities of
Bakunin since his return from Russia: 'While allowing complete liberty
to the movements and the aspirations of the working class in the
various countries, the International has nevertheless succeeded in
uniting it into one body, and for the first time making the ruling classes
and their governments feel the cosmopolitan power of the proletariat
. . . And this is the moment chosen by the members of the Alliance to
declare open war on the General Council . . . Their resounding phrases
on autonomy and free federation, in a word, their war cries, against the
General Council were therefore only a manoeuvre to mask their true
end: to disorganise the International and in this way even to subject
it to the secret hierarchical and aristocratic government of the Alliance.'
(July 21) Foreseeing that the IWMA Congress arranged for September
in Geneva would end in failure, Marx and Engels decide to refrain
from all participation and persuade their closest friends to follow
their example. The General Council having been unable to send a
single delegate to Geneva, the 'anti-authoritarians' constitute themselves
as the sixth Congress of the IWMA and recognise the necessity of the
political struggle of the working class. Marx writes to Sorge, after the
Geneva fiasco: 'In my opinion, in the present situation in Europe, it
will be very useful for the moment to leave in the background the
formal organisation of the International . . . . Events and the inevitable
development of things will themselves do what is necessary for the
rebirth of the International.' (September 27) Bakunin calls Marx a
'police informer and slanderer,' (September 26) and publicly announces
his retirement from public life and his resignation from the International (Letter to the Jurassian Federation (October)). Darwin thanks
Marx for sending him *Capital*: 'Though our studies have been so
different, I believe that we both earnestly desire the extension of
knowledge, and that this in the long run is sure to add to the happiness
of mankind.' (October 1) Visit to Harrogate for a cure, accompanied
by Eleanor (November 24–December 15). The doctor forbids him all
activity. Engels reads the manuscript of the French translation of some
pages of *Capital* and regrets that 'the form and vigour of the original are

lacking'. (to Marx, November 29) Marx on Saint-Beuve's *Chateau-briand*: 'If this author has become so famous in France it is because he is in all respects the classical incarnation of French vanity: this vanity does not wear the soft and frivolous clothing of the 18th century, but a romantic costume; it struts about in modernistic phraseology, false profundity, byzantine exaggeration, sentimental coquetry, the brilliant and the gaudy, theatrical and exalted verbal colouring – in a word, a concoction of lies that has never been equalled in form or in content.' (to Engels, November 30)

1874

Notes on Bakunin: 'Statism and Anarchy'

January-May: For Book III of *Capital* Marx collects material on agrarian problems: the physiology of plants and the chemistry of fertilisers. With regard to the information given in the German press on the gravity of his illness: 'Nothing annoys me so much as to look as if I am issuing reports to the public through my friends . . . on my state of health. I don't care a rap for the public and if my temporary relapses are exaggerated, that at least has the advantage of sparing me all sorts of requests (theoretical and other) coming from unknown persons.' (January 19) Liebknecht asks Marx and Engels to have *Poverty of Philosophy* and *The Holy Family* reprinted through the good offices of the *Volkstaat* publishing house. Marx studies the English blue books on the recent history of English economic policy. He receives a visit from P L Lavrov, a Russian populist and editor of the review *Vpered* (Zurich and London) To cure himself of insomnia he stays in Ramsgate for several weeks. His doctor advises complete rest and a cure at Karlsbad. Resumption of work on revising the French translation of *Capital* (May-July). To Kugelmann: 'The progress of the labour movement in Germany (and in Austria) is very satisfactory. In France, the absence of theoretical foundations and political good sense is generally felt. In England, it is only in the rural labour movement that there is progress; the industrial workers must first of all get rid of their present leaders.' (May 18)

June-December: Marx and Engels are alarmed by the sympathy shown to the economist Eugen Dühring in German social democratic circles.

They advise the leaders of the German Social Democratic Party of their fears. A fortnight's rest in Ryde (July 15-30). Marx applies for English citizenship but recevieves a negative response from the Home Secretary. who does not however make public the reason for his refusal. ('This man has failed in loyalty to his king') (August). On announcing his approaching departure for Karlsbad, Marx writes to Sorge: 'They tell me that when I get back I shall have recovered my full working capacity: truly, to be unable to work is a death sentence for any man who is not an animal.' With regard to Germany and Europe: 'In Germany Bismarck is working for us. The general situation in Europe is such that it is advancing farther and farther toward a European war. We must pass through that before one can think of any effective and decisive action by the working class in Europe.' (August 4) Marx and Eleanor go to Karlsbad to take the waters there. (August 19-September 21) Frequent conversations with Kugelmann, for whom Marx's affection is cooling. On the way back, Marx stops in Dresden, Leipzig, Berlin and Hamburg. In Leipzig he meets Liebknecht and local representatives of the party. Reprinting by the *Volkstaat* of the *Revelations on the Trial of the Cologne Communists* (October-January 1855). Marx and Engels are informed of the negotiations between the Lassallean and the Social Democratic parties with a view to unification. (October) In the course of 1874, Marx reads numerous Russian books, among them Bakunin's *Statism and Anarchy* (Geneva 1873) in which Marx has a prominent place as a Jew and a state socialist. His critical annotations enable him to clarify his ideas of revolutions in predominantly peasant countries and of the dictatorship of the proletariat in Western countries.

1875

Revelations on the Trial of the Cologne Communists (New edition with postface)
Le Capital Livre I. (French edition)
Critique of the programme of the German Workers' Party (The Gotha Programme)

January-July: Postface to the reimpression of *Revelations* . . .: 'The trial of the Cologne Communists brands the impotence of the state power in its struggle against social development . . . Society will only achieve its equilibrium on the day it finds its centre of gravity: labour.'

(January 8) Marx and Engels speak at a meeting in honour of the Polish insurrection of 1863-1864. There Marx explains the reasons for the labour party's interest in the fate of Poland: sympathy with the oppressed people, the geographical, military and historical position of Poland, and above all: 'Poland is not merely the only Slav nation, but also the only European people which has fought and still fights as a cosmopolitan soldier of the revolution.' (January 23) Marx sends Engels the pamphlet by the populist P Tkachev, *Open Letter to Mr F Engels* (Zurich 1874), asking him to publish a reply. Engels does so by writing as essay entitled *The Social Question in Russia* (*Volkstaat* March-April) in which he attacks the belief in Russia's special vocation for socialism before the triumph of a proletarian revolution in the West. 'This man, who claims that the revolution could be achieved more easily in his country because the latter has neither proletariat nor bourgeoisie, proves by that very argument that he has not understood anything about socialism.' For the French edition of *Capital* Marx writes a foreword in which he stresses that the French version of his work possesses an independent scientific value. (April 28) At the request of W Bracke, a leading member of the German Social Democratic Party and a Reichstag deputy, Marx sets out in *Marginal Notes* his views on the programme of the German Social Democratic Party and of the Lassallean party (the so-called *Gotha Programme*) He opposes to the Lassallean 'free state' the view that the period of transition from capitalist to communist society will necessitate 'the revolutionary dictatorship of the proletariat.' (May 5) He maintains close relations with P Lavrov, to whom he writes in a letter concerning the experiments of the physiologist Traube, who was said to have succeeded in creating artificial cells: 'It is a great step forward, specially considering that Helmholz and others began to proclaim the absurd thesis that the germs of life on earth originated on the moon and were brought by meteorites. I hate explanations that solve problems by removing them to an unknown region.' (June 18)

August-December: Another visit to Karlsbad for a cure. There Marx frequently sees Maxim Kovalevsky, a Russian historian. On his return from Karlsbad, he stops in Prague where he meets Max Oppenheim, the democratic publicist. (September 11-13) On *A Few Words from a Revolutionary Socialist Group*, a pamphlet by a Bakunist, he writes: 'This schoolboy exercise doesn't deserve a reply'. (to Lavrov, October 8) In agreement with Marx, Engels in his letters to Bracke and Bebel returns to the question of the unity congress and the Gotha programme. He considers this, in its definitive form, as a document in the spirit of Lassalle, enriched with a few misunderstood and distorted arguments from the *Communist Manifesto*: 'Fortunately, the programme has been received more favourably than it deserves. Workers, bourgeois and petty-bourgeois read in it what they choose to find, and what in fact is not there. . . This has allowed us to remain silent.' Further: 'Marx has returned from Karlsbad completely changed: robust, cheerful, lively and in good health, so he will soon be able to start work again.' (to Bracke, October 11) With regard to the formula in the Eisenach programme on 'the aid given by the state to the co-operative movement,' which is reproduced in the Gotha programme: 'State aid as conceived by Lassalle certainly figured in the Eisenach programme, but only as one of the temporary measures . . . And now it makes its appearance as the unique and universal remedy for all social ills.' (to Bebel, October 12) Lachatre publishes the last part of the French edition of *Capital*. Marx sends a number of copies to his relations and friends (end of November). He resumes his Russian reading and continues to assemble a mass of publications relating to economic and social problems in Russia (agronomy, landed property, the fiscal system, the money market, etc.) Marx is invited by Lavrov to speak at a Polish meeting, but he is suffering from a boil on the chest and cannot attend: 'Besides, I could only repeat the opinion I have defended for 30 years: the liberation of Poland is one of the conditions for the liberation of the working class in Europe. The conspiracies of the Holy Alliance give new proofs of this.' (December 3)

1876

Speech on the Communist League

January–July: Speech by Marx at a commemorative celebration of the German Cultural Association in London. He outlines the history of the Communist League, going back to the League of the Just whose international character he emphasises. (February 7) In relation to the problems of Book III of *Capital*, Marx writes a series of comments on 'differential rent and rent as interest on capital embodied in the land.' Studies of vegetable, animal and human physiology (Schleiden, Ranke). From Budapest Leo Frankel informs Marx of his arrest in Vienna and his declarations before an examining magistrate on the subject of his participation in the Commune (March 18). Marx asks Sorge to obtain for him American library catalogues since 1843; he wants to acquaint himself with the literature that has appeared in the US on agriculture, landed property and credit. (April 4) He also corresponds with Leo Frankel in order to study the same problems in Hungary. (May) He sends Sorge the second edition of *Capital and Labour* (Chemnitz 1876), an abridged version of *Capital* made by Johann Most with the author's help. '. . . I have not put my name to it, because there would still have been many things to change (I had to eliminate various pages on value, money, wage labour, etc. entirely, and replace them with my own texts).' (June 14) Marx and Engels agree to oppose the growing influence of Eugen Dühring's ideas in certain social democratic circles. Engels begins to assemble materials to his end. To Marx: 'You have given me a fine job. You can stay in your nice warm bed, busy yourself with Russian agriculture in general and ground rent in particular, while I have to sit on a hard bench, drink cold wine, and suddenly interrupt everything in order to look for lice on the head of that tedious Dühring.' He outlines the plan of the book they have in mind. (May 28) Marx and Engels are annoyed by the compliments paid in the socialist press (*Vpered*, *Volkstaat*) to Bakunin, who had died on July 1. (July 25 and 26)

August–December: Departure for Karlsbad with Eleanor. Telling Engels about the ups and downs of his journey, Marx describes the crowds making for Bayreuth for 'the festival of the fans of Wagner, the State musician.' At the hotel, he finds a book sent by Lavrov, *The State Element in the Future Society*: 'Anyway, I am putting off reading this to the future. Here, everything is in the future, beginning with the noise of the music of the future at Bayreuth.' (August 19) To his daughter Jenny Longuet: 'Everywhere we go they weary us with the question: What do you think of Wagner? Very typical for this neo–German–Prussian national musician: he and his wife (divorced by Bülow), the cuckold Bülow, and the father-in-law they have in common, Liszt; all four live together in perfect accord, coaxing, hugging and mutually adoring each other and leading a pleasant life. Moreover, when one thinks that Liszt is a monk and Madame Wagner (her name is Cosima) is his "natural" daughter, a gift from Madame d'Agoult (Daniel Stern) . . . one couldn't imagine a better libretto for an Offenbach opera than this family group with its patriarchal relations. One could represent its deeds and gestures, like those of the Nibelungen, in a tetralogy.' (September) On the way back Marx and Eleanor make a stop in Kreuznach where Marx recalls for his daughter his memories of the time when he was newly married. In a letter to Liebknecht Marx disapproves of the attempts to reconcile social democracy with the anarchists 'who have worked for the dissolution of the International.' On the occasion of new complications in the East, he insists on the necessity for discussing the Eastern question again, and for denouncing the policy of Bismarck, who 'is flirting officially with Russia.' 'By his policy of conquest in France, Bismarck has disarmed Germany in relation to Russia, condemning her to the infamous role she is playing now, which is truly the shame of Europe.' On the other hand, there is a change of policy in England, where Gladstone and Russell are beating a retreat, while the most enlightened workers are agitating against the Russophile proletarians. 'I think, in fact, that it is your duty to write an editorial unmasking the bourgeois press, itself Germano-Russian, which pretends to be anti-Russian, allows itself at the most a few liberties with foreign ministries, but closes its mouth religiously on the subject of its own Bismarck.' (October 7) Liebknecht will publish in *Vorwärts* a series of polemical articles on European policy toward Russia. With respect to Laveleye's article on *Capital* in the *Revue des deux mondes*: 'You need to have read it in order to get an idea of the idiocy of our bourgeois "thinkers". M Laveleye is nevertheless sufficiently naive to acknowledge that if one accepts the doctrines of Adam Smith and Ricardo or even – *horrible dictu* – the doctrines of Carey and Bastiat, one cannot avoid the erroneous conclusions of *Capital*.' (To Lavrov, October 7) Marx sends to Charles D Collet, a follower of Urquhart, information on Gladstone's Russian policy which the publicist will use in his articles for the *Diplomatic Review*. Maxim Kovalevsky is a constant visitor to the Marx family.

1877

Articles opposing Gladstone's Russophile policy
Marginal Notes on 'Critical History'
Russia's Social Future

January–July: Marx continues his reading on Russia throughout the year; principally on the condition of agriculture since the abolition of serfdom. He follows closely the development of the Russo-Turkish conflict. In a letter from Jenny Marx: 'My husband is at present up to his neck in the Eastern question, and rejoices to see the firm and honourable attitude of the sons of Mahomet in face of all the Christian double-dealing and the hypocrisies of the atrocity-monger.' (to Sorge, 20) Marx is delighted with the electoral successes of the Social Democrats. 'The Eastern question (which will end in a revolution in Russia, whatever the result of the war against the Turks) and the mobilisation of the social democratic forces in the fatherland, will have convinced the cultured Philistine in Germany that there are more important things in the world than Wagner's *Zukunftsmusik* (music of the future).' (to Dr Freund, January 21) Through the mediation of M Barry, Marx conducts a press campaign against Gladstone's pro-Russia policy. The articles appear anonymously in several conservative journals. (February and March) Correspondence with the historian of Judaism, H Graetz, with whom Marx had formed a friendship at Karlsbad. Graetz thanks Marx for sending him *Capital* and other writings. On the *Address on the Commune* he says: 'When a man like you speaks these words (Paris the whole truth, Versailles all lies) it is as if the last judgment of history has pronounced the verdict.' (February 1) For Engels' *Anti-Dühring* Marx writes the chapter on Dühring's critical history of political economy. He asks Lavrov for a brief account of the persecutions by the judiciary and the police in Russia: this information is intended for an Irish MP with a view to a speech on the subject of the 'Commission on Reforms' appointed by the Russian government for Turkey. (March 16) Correspondence with W Bracke about the German translation of Lissagaray's *History of the Commune* which Marx is revising. Marx begins a new draft of Book II of *Capital*. He writes to Bracke: 'The working class press is too little concerned with the Eastern question and forgets that government policy is playing arrogantly with the life and wealth of the people.' (April 21) Marx refuses to contribute to some new German reviews which seem to him pseudo-scientific: 'To be uncompromising – the first condition of all criticism – is impossible in such company; besides, I should have to be trying all the time to be easily understandable; in other words, to write for the ignorant. Imagine a journal of chemistry in which one had to assume from the start the reader's ignorance of chemistry.' (to Engels, July 18) With regard to the strikes in the US: 'This first explosion against the oligarchy associated with capital will undoubtedly be crushed, but it may well be the starting-point for a genuine workers' party in the US.' (to Engels, July 25)

August–December: Marx assembles various writings by Owen for the

chapter on socialism in Engels' *Anti-Dühring*. Marx, his sick wife and
Eleanor go to stay at Neuenahr and in the Black Forest (August–
September). With regard to the crisis in the East: 'This crisis is a new
turning-point in European history. Russia, whose condition I have
studied in the original Russian sources, official and non-official, . . . has
been on the brink of an upheaval for a long time; all the elements are
ready . . . All strata of Russian society are in decay, economically,
morally and intellectually. This time the revolution is starting in the
East, where the hitherto unshattered bastion, and the reserve army of
counter-revolution are situated.' (to Sorge, September 27) Following
the compromise between the Social Democrats and the Lassalleans,
dubious intellectual elements have streamed into the Germany party,
who would like to give socialism a 'superior and ideal' direction; in
other words, 'to replace the materialist basis (which requires serious
objective study if one wants to make use of it) by the modern mythology with its goddesses of justice, liberty, equality and fraternity.'
(to Sorge, October 19) On the subject of the 'cult of personality',
Marx recalls, in a letter to W Blos, that at the time of the International
he and Engels had frustrated all the manoeuvres intended to trap them
in the toils of publicity. 'When Engels and I first entered the secret
society of the communists, we did so on condition that the statutes
excluded everything which might encourage trust in authority.'
(November 10) Marx drafts a reply (posthumously published) to N
Mikhailovsky, a Russian sociologist and populist who had attributed
to him the theory that in order to attain socialism, Russia must first
plunge into capitalism and get rid of the rural commune. He denies
propounding 'a historical–philosophical theory of a universal movement necessarily imposed upon all peoples whatever the historical
circumstances in which they are placed . . .' But 'if Russia strives to
develop as a capitalist nation on the pattern of the nations of Western
Europe . . . she will not succeed without having first transformed a
good part of her peasants into proletarians; and once drawn into the
whirlwind of the capitalist economy she will be subject to its inexor-
able laws, just like the other secular nations.' (November)

1878

Two Letters on the Eastern Question
Against Lothar Bucher

Mr George Howell's History of the IWMA
The Anti-Socialist Law

January–August: In two letters to Wilhelm Liebknecht, the spokesman
in *Vorwärts!* for the anti-Russian tendency in social democracy, Marx
says what he thinks (in agreement with Engels) about the Russo-
Turkish conflict and its immediate and long term repercussions on the
political and social situation in Europe: 'We are strongly on the side of
the Turkish peasant for two reasons: first, because we have studied the
Turkish peasant, that is, the mass of the Turkish people, and have
understood that he is undoubtedly one of the most valiant and moral
representatives of European peasantry; second, because the defeat of
Russia would have accelerated greatly a social upheaval in Russia, and
at the same time an upheaval throughout Europe. Things have taken
a different turn. Why? Because of the treachery of England and
Austria.' (February 4) If the Russian peace conditions are accepted, the
longer term result will be a European war which will bring about a
social crisis and mark the end of the military powers, led by Prussia.
In his second letter Marx points to the demoralisation of the English
working class since 1848 and the venality of its Russophile leaders:
'but the rapid development of the Russian projects has suddenly
broken the spell' and these leaders no longer dare to make their voices
heard in workers' meetings. (February 11) Liebknecht publishes
Marx's letters as an appendix to the second edition of his pamphlet
The Eastern Question or Will Europe become Cossack? Marx is informed of the activities of Jules Guesde and the difficulties encoun-
tered in the publication of the journal *Égalité*. In a notebook of more
than 300 pages, he annotates excerpts from I I Kaufmann's work
(in Russian), *Theory and Practice of Banking* (Vol I Petersburg, 1873).
Throughout the year he will study the problems of money, agronomy
and geology, reading a number of historical and theoretical works (P
Rota, G Perrot, L Cossa, Charles A Mann, A Walker, C D Hüllmann,
J Grassiot, etc., J B Jukes, J F W Johnston, J G Koppe, etc.). In the
press Marx denounces Bismarck's measures against social democracy
following the attempts on the life of William I by Hödel and Nobiling.
In several open letters he calls on Lothar Bucher (a former disciple of
Lassalle, follower of Urquhart and member of the International, who
has become Bismarck's right-hand man) to declare publicly that the
doctrines of the German socialist party have nothing to do with these
attempts. (June 12) Following a polemical article by G Howell, a
former member of the Federal Council of the IWMA, on the history of

the International and the role played in it by Marx, the latter publishes a reply: he corrects errors of fact committed by Howell and defends the memory of the IWMA against his slanderous allegations. The IWMA has acquired a world wide reputation and a place in the history of humanity not as a result of a well-supplied treasury, but through its spiritual force and disinterested energy. In spite of its formal dissolution, the International is not dead; on the contrary, it has entered a higher stage since its aspirations have been in part realised. In the course of its progressive development it will have to go through many metamorphoses before the last chapter of its history is written. (July) The first edition of *Anti-Dühring* is published in Leipzig. In the introduction, Engels observes 'These two great discoveries, the materialist conception of history and the revelation of the secret of capitalist production through surplus value, are due to Marx. With him socialism became a science, which it is now a question of elaborating in all its details.'

September–December: Marx goes to stay in Malvernbury where his sick wife is taking the cure. There he meets Kovalevsky, who tells him about the University of Moscow where Montenegrin students 'acquire a fanatical hatred of the Russians.' They say: 'Russians in general, and Russian students in particular, patronise us as if we were barbarians and ruffians; so the Russian government achieves the opposite of what it is trying to do with its scholarships.' (to Engels, September 17) On the occasion of the debates in the Reichstag on the Anti-Socialist Law the Minister of the Interior refers to the 'Marx tendency' which he compares with anarchism, and Marx collects material for an article he intends to send to the *Daily News*, but does not complete it. With reference to a remark made by the Minister concerning the ideas of social democracy on the use of violence in the pursuit of its aims, Marx notes: 'For us, the aim is the emancipation of the working class and the social transformation which that involves. A historical development can only remain "peaceful" as long as it does not encounter violent opposition from the holders of power in society. If, for example, the working class in England or the USA were one day to have a majority in Parliament or Congress, it would be able to eliminate laws and institutions by legal means . . . Nevertheless, the "peaceful" movement might be transformed into "violence" if those who have an interest in the former state of things rebel; if they are conquered by *force* (as in the American Civil War and the French Revolution) it is as rebels against the legal power.' (September 24) Marx supplies information to M Kaufmann for his book *Utopias; or Schemes of Social Improvement, from Sir Thomas More to Karl Marx* (London 1879). Marx lets Danielson know that Book II of *Capital* will be ready for printing toward the end of 1879. He tells him about the economic prospects in the United States, especially the enormous development of industry and commerce which has substituted for negro slavery the slavery of white workers. (November 15) Marx reads some studies of Leibniz, and also Descartes' posthumously published writings on physics and mathematics. Jules Guesde replies to a letter from Marx and says he is in agreement with him on essentials. 'If I am a revolutionary, and like you believe in the necessity of force to solve the social question in a collectivist or communist way, I am also, as you are, a resolute opponent of movements such as Cafiero's which may be useful in Russia but which do not correspond to any requirement of the situation in France, Germany or Italy . . . Like you, I am convinced that before thinking of action, a party and a conscious army must have been established by means of active and continuous propaganda. Like you, I deny that the simple destruction of what exists is sufficient for the building of what we desire and I think that for a fairly long time the impulse and direction will have to come from above, from those who "know more". This being so, I have been occupied since my return in forming the "independent and militant labour party" which you so rightly say is "of the greatest importance in view of coming events".' (December 1878– January 1879)

1879

Circular Letter to the Social Democratic Leaders

January–August: Marx receives a visit from Sir Mountstuart E Grant-Duff, a liberal MP. In a letter to the Empress Frederika of Germany, reporting the conversation with Marx, this English diplomat writes: 'It was all very *positif*, slightly cynical – without any appearance of enthusiasm – interesting and often, as I thought, showing very correct ideas when he was conversing of the past and the present, but vague and unsatisfactory when he turned to the future. (. . .)

' "But supposing," I said, "the rulers of Europe came to an understanding amongst themselves for a reduction of armaments which might greatly relieve the burden on the people, what would become of the

Revolution which you expect it one day to bring about?"

' "Ah", was his answer, "they can't do that. All sorts of fears and jealousies will make that impossible. The burden will grow worse and worse as science advances, for the improvements in the Art of Destruction will keep pace with its advance and every year more and more will have to be devoted to costly engines of war. It is a vicious circle – there is no escape from it." (. . .)

'The above will give Your Imperial Highness a fair idea of the kind of ideas about the near future of Europe which are working in his mind.

'They are too dreamy to be dangerous, except just in so far as the situation with its mad expenditure on armaments is obviously and undoubtedly dangerous.' (February 1) Jenny Marx's illness becomes worse. Marx's health also deteriorates and his capacity for work is diminished. Commenting on a letter from Danielson on Russia's financial policy during the last 15 years and alluding to a passage in which his correspondent compares the economic development of America and Russia, Marx shows the lack of substance in his comparison: 'In the former the expenses of the government diminish daily and its public debt is quickly and yearly reduced; in the latter bankruptcy is a goal more and more appearing to become unavoidable. The former has freed itself . . . of its paper money, the latter has no more flourishing fabric than that of paper money . . . the latter reminds you rather of the times of Louis XIV and Louis XV . . .' America is exceeding even England's tempo of industrial development, and its masses are more dynamic and endowed with greater political means to achieve their goals. With regards to Book II of *Capital*, Marx declares that he will not publish it before having seen the development and outcome of the industrial crisis in England. (April 10) The libertarian Carlo Cafiero, who in 1872 had combatted the General Council of the IWMA, sends Marx the *Précis of Capital* which he wrote during his imprisonment. Marx thanks him (in French) and praises the pamphlet, while pointing out an omission in the preface, 'namely, the proof that the necessary material conditions for the emancipation of the proletariat are generated spontaneously by the process of capitalist exploitation.' (July 29) Marx and Engels are extremely busy with a plan to create an illegal journal of social democracy. Having at first promised their collaboration in the *Sozialdemokrat*, they later withdraw it, having learned that the journal's programme would not be proletarian and revolutionary, but inspired by a philanthropic and opportunist outlook. (Engels to Bebel, August 4) Marx takes a holiday in Ramsgate.

September–December: At Marx's request, Engels writes on behalf of both of them a circular letter addressed to the leaders of the Social Democratic Party; in which he condemns the opportunism manifest in the programme of their journal, planned and worked out by bourgeois intellectuals; for these people, who despise the proletarian masses, 'the working class by itself is incapable of liberating itself; it must therefore come under the sway of members of the educated and well-to-do bourgeoisie who alone have the opportunity and the time to make themselves familiar with the interests of the workers.' The revolutionary programme is postponed and in its place humble submission to the government and the bourgeoisie, which one wants to win over and convince, is advocated. The class struggle is set aside and replaced by appeals to love and justice. 'As for us, after all our past experience, only one path remains open to us. For nearly 40 years, we have pointed to the class struggle as the most decisive motive force of history, and have indicated that the social struggle between the bourgeoisie and the proletariat is the great lever of the modern social revolution . . . At the time of the creation of the International we formulated the slogan for our struggle: "the emancipation of the working class will be the work of the working class itself." Consequently, we cannot make common cause with people who openly desire that workers are too uncultivated to liberate themselves and that they must be freed from above, that is, by the lower and upper middle class philanthropists.' (September 17) In a letter to Sorge, Marx describes in detail the relations that he and Engels maintain with J Most and his journal *Die Freiheit* and their disputes with the social democratic leaders on the subject of the new anarchist journal. On the socialist deputies: '. . . These gentlemen are already so affected by parliamentary cretinism that they believe themselves to be above criticism and reject it as a crime of lèse-majesté.' (September 19) Further Russian readings, including Kovalevsky's *Rural Communal Ownership* and the documents on Russian finances sent by Danielson. Achille Loria sends Marx his work on *Ground Rent* and tells him in a letter that he owes his method of research to Marx (November 23). Studies of ancient history especially in the field of Roman civilisation and law. In an interview granted to the correspondent of the *Chicago Tribune* Marx speaks of the necessity of an independent working class party in America; socialists participate in the movement but they are not its initiators; they 'merely tell the workmen what its character and its ends will be". (December 18, published January 5, 1879)

1880

Questionnaire for an Investigation of Workers (Enquête ouvrière)
Preamble to the Programme of the French Workers' Party
Marginal Notes on Adolph Wagner's 'Manual of Political Economy'
Chronological Notes on India

January–December: During the whole of the year Marx will be working intermittently on Volumes II and III of *Capital* and reading books on ground rent (A Loris), geology (G Allen) and financial questions. He receives a visit from Paul Brousse, the future leader of the 'possibilists' (March). For the benefit of the French socialists Marx drafts a questionnaire of a hundred items with a view to an enquiry to be conducted among workers on their economic, social and political situation. (April) *L'Égalité*, a journal edited by J Guesde, reprints parts of *Poverty of Philosophy*. Guesde and Lafargue meet at Engels' home, and in the presence of Marx discuss the programme of the French workers' party. At Marx's dictation, Guesde writes the *Preamble to the Programme* (May) where it is stated that the organisation of the working class into an independent political party 'should be pursued by all the means available to the proletariat, including universal suffrage, which is thus transformed, from the instrument of deception which it has been hitherto, into an instrument of emancipation.' Marx writes a foreword for the French edition of *Socialism, Utopian and Scientific*. This excerpt from Engels' *Anti-Dühring* forms what might be called an 'introduction to scientific socialism'. (May) Marx authorises Domela Nieuwenhuis, a pioneer of Dutch socialism, to publish a popular summary of *Capital* in Dutch. Visit of the Marx family, including the two sons-in-law, to Ramsgate (August–September). To Danielson: '. . . I should be happy if I could be of use to you but . . . at the moment I am not able to do any theoretical work. The doctors have sent me here "to do nothing", in order to cure my nerves.' Marx authorises him to use, for his *Sketches of the Russian Economy*, whatever he might find worthwhile in the letters Marx had sent to him. He expresses the hope that there will not be a general war in Europe. 'Even though it cannot hold up the ultimate effects of social, – I mean economic – development, and on the contrary may even intensify this development, it could certainly entail a useless expenditure of strength over a long period.' (September 12) Liebknecht pays a visit to Marx and Engels and discusses with them problems of the party and also of the *Sozialdemokrat*, whose opportunist attitude he pledges himself to change. H M Hyndman makes frequent visits to Marx with whom he discusses the creation of a workers' party in England. In a letter to Sorge Marx gives an account of the unpleasant dealings he and Engels have had with Johann Most on the one hand and the socialists of Leipzig on the other. He also informs him of the progress of 'modern scientific, that is to say German, socialism' in France, where Lafargue has become 'one of the most influential writers in *Justice*, the journal of Clemenceau, leader of the extreme left.' And in conclusion, he speaks of 'our success' in Russia, 'where *Capital* is read and recognised more than anywhere else.' He indicates his sympathy for the Russian terrorists who are risking their lives in Russia while the 'so-called party of propaganda' resides in Geneva and opposes all political and revolutionary action, believing that 'Russia will arrive in one perilous leap in the anarchist–communist–atheist millenium.' (November 5) The executive committee of the Russian revolutionary party *Narodnaya Volya* pays tribute to Marx's work and asks him to use his influence to arouse sympathy in Europe and America for the revolutionary movement in Russia. Marx maintains friendly relations with Léon Hartmann, a delegate of the Rusian party, established in London since March 1880. Marx, Engels, Lessner and Lafargue address a letter to the meeting convened in Geneva to commemorate the 50th anniversary of the Polish revolution of 1830. They recall that the Polish insurrection of 1863 was the starting point for the foundation of the International. (November 17) In a letter to Hyndmann – who had told him that he did not share the views of his party on England – Marx declares that this party does not regard an English revolution as necessary but, in the light of historical precedents, possible. 'If the inevitable evolution turns into a revolution, it would be the fault not only of the ruling classes, but of the working class as well.' Any peaceful concession by the former was torn from them by 'external pressure'. Their action corresponded with this pressure, and if the latter became ever weaker it is because the English working class does not know how to use the power and the liberties which it certainly possesses. He goes on to point out that the workers in Germany have understood that only a revolution could set them free from military despotism, but that it was necessary first to organise and educate themselves and thus remain within the bounds of legality. 'The illegality was on the government's side, for it has outlawed the working class.' (December 8) The Narodnik Morozov pays a visit to Marx to inform him about the causes of the split in the *Zemlya i Volya* party, and about the struggle against Tsarist autocracy. For several months Marx has been reading Adolph Wagner's *Manual of*

Political Economy and annotating the passages which the author
devotes to *Capital*, especially to the so-called 'socialist system' of Marx
and its 'corner-stone', the theory of value.

1881

Annotated Excerpts from L H Morgan's 'Ancient Society'
The Future of the Russian Rural Commune

January–March: Reading of Russian works. Marx studies the development of the Russian economy since the emancipation of the serfs
(Skrebitsky, Golovachov, Skaldin, Danielson, Janson, Chernychevsky).
He provides Longuet with information for articles in *Justice* on the
political career of Charles Bradlaugh, a radical journalist on the staff of
the *National Reformer*, who in 1871 had attacked the General Council
of the IWMA and the Communards: 'in the last elections Bradlaugh ...
was one of the most clamorous supporters of Gladstone's demagogic
Russophile campaign against Disraeli.' (January 4) Marx is visited by
the Russian economists Sieber and Kablukov. He corresponds with E
Fortin, who proposes to publish a precis of *Capital* and to translate the
Critique of 1859, for he would like to 'inundate France with streams of
light'. (to Longuet, January 4) Vera Zasulich, a member of the revolutionary group called 'the Black Partition', known for her attempt on
the life of the Prefect of Petersburg, Trepov, in 1878 (she was acquitted
at her trial) is in Geneva. She asks Marx to set out his views on the
social future of Russia; will the country have to suffer the fate of the
Western countries, as 'Marxists' claim and pass through the state of
capitalism before reaching socialism, or will it be able to avoid this
fate by making the rural commune the foundation of a communal
society such as the populists (Narodniks) desire? 'The personal destiny
of our revolutionary socialists depends upon the way in which this
question is viewed.' (February 16) Marx praises Danielson's *Sketches*
and encourages him to persevere by studying especially the problem of
the indebtedness of owners in Russia. He outlines the relationship
between the public debt and railway construction in England and the
USA. He comments on the revolts which are in store for the English
government in India as a result of the savage exploitation of the
workers. (to Danielson, February 19) In reply to a question posed by
Domela Nieuwenhuis, Marx says that he considers it a mistake to ask

118

oneself questions about the measures which a socialist government would have to take after the 'victory': 'A socialist government will not come to the helm of the ship of state unless conditions are sufficiently developed to enable it first of all to take the measures necessary for striking fear into the bourgeoisie so as to secure for itself the main advantage — time for effective action.' One should not invoke here the example of the Commune which, existing in a single town, did not and could not have a socialist majority. 'The doctrinal, and necessarily imaginative anticipation of the programme of action for a future revolution only diverts attention from the present struggle. The dream of the imminent destruction of the world inspired the early Christians and gave them the certainty of victory. The scientific understanding of the inevitable and increasingly visible decay of the prevailing social order, the growing hatred of the masses for the old phantoms who are in power, and the simultaneous huge development of the means of production — all that is a guarantee that at the moment when a real proletarian revolution breaks out there will also appear the conditions (certainly far from idyllic) in which it will carry out its most urgent immediate measures.' (February 22) Stimulated by Vera Zasulich's letter, Marx outlines a sociological study (written in French) of the economic development of Russia. The peculiarities of its economic and social structure exclude the possibility of applying directly the lessons that can be drawn from an analysis of Western capitalism. Under certain conditions (and first of all the condition of a revolution) the rural commune in Russia can become the starting point for a socialist transformation, 'the regenerative element of Russian society'. Severely afflicted by illness, Marx is unable to present this sketch in a definitive form, and confines himself to a brief reply which concludes thus: 'The analysis in *Capital*, therefore, does not offer arguments either for or against the vitality of the rural commune, but the special study I have made of it, based upon material from the original sources, has convinced me that the commune is the basis for social regeneration in Russia. But in order that it should function in this way it would be necessary first to eliminate the harmful influences that assail it from all sides and then to ensure normal conditions for its spontaneous development.' (March 8) In a letter addressed to the meeting of Slavs to commemorate the anniversary of the Paris Commune, organised in London under the chairmanship of Leon Hartmann, Marx and Engels interpret the assassination of Tsar Alexander II as presaging the inevitable occurrence of a 'Russian Commune'. (March 21)

119

April–December: A qualified judgment by Marx on Karl Kautsky, after their first meeting. (letter to Jenny Longuet, April 11) With reference to the terrorists tried in Petersburg: 'These are people of extraordinary ability, without any melodramatic affectation; simple, solid, heroic. Shouting and acting are two fundamentally irreconcilable things. The Petersburg Executive Committee, whose actions are so vigorous, publishes subtly "moderate" manifestos far removed from the school-boy manner of people like Most and other infantile loud-mouths, who preach tyrannicide as a "theory" and a "panacea" . . . they try on the contrary to teach Europe that their method of action is specifically Russian and historically inevitable, which it is as useless to moralise about — either for or against — as about the Chios earthquake.' (to Jenny, April 11) Readings about America (large scale industry, monopolies, child labour, etc.). After the birth of Marcel Longuet; '. . . I prefer the masculine sex for children who are born at this turning-point of history. They have before them the most revolutionary period that men have ever had to go through. What is sad today is to be old, so that one can only foresee rather than see.' (to Jenny, April 29) Harsh judgment on Henry George's *Progress and Poverty*. Marx ranges the state control of ground rent with those necessarily contradictory transitional measures which may lead to socialism; nationalised rent is only a disguised way of saving the capitalist class and even extending the basis of its rule, as long as wage labour continues. (Marx to Sorge, June 20) In his book *England for All*, Hyndman includes long excerpts from *Capital* without naming either the author or his book, on the pretext that Marx's name is too much detested by the English. Marx breaks with Hyndman (July). Visit by Marx and his wife to the Longuets at Argenteuil (July 26–August 16). Marx undertakes some historical reading (the French Revolution, colonial peoples). On the political situation in France: 'It is possible that the extreme left is grow-ing slightly in numbers, but the principal result will probably be the victory of Gambetta. Considering French conditions, the short electoral period will award the decision to the schemers who hold the key positions, to those who will probably dispense jobs in the government machine and who have state funds at their disposal.' (to Engels, August 9) Engels studies Marx's notebooks on Mathematics and compliments his friend on the clarity of his method of expounding the differential calculus. (August 18) Lissagaray gives Marx information on the situa-tion of the workers' party and the dissensions among its leaders. (to Engels, August 18) Marx falls gravely ill (peritonitis and bronchitis). Since her return from Paris his wife has been obliged to take to her bed, suffering from cancer of the liver, and never gets up again. She dies on December 2. On the preceding day, the review *Modern Thought*, in a series of studies entitled 'Leaders of Modern Thought' has devoted an article, written by Belfort Bax, to Marx, who was able to show it to his dying wife, thereby 'enlightening her final moments'. Engels, at the grave of Jenny Marx: 'If ever a woman found her greatest happiness in making others happy, it was she.' (December 15) 'I emerge from my latest illness doubly maimed, morally by the death of my wife, and physically as a result of a thickening of the pleura and an increased irritability of the bronchia.' (Marx to Sorge, December 15) The doctor had forbidden him to attend his wife's funeral. 'I am resigned, because the night before she died, the dear departed said again to the nurse, alluding to the possible omission of some ceremony: "We are not people who cling to outward show" . . . There is only one antidote against mental suffering: namely, physical pain. Let the end of the world be confronted by a man with raging toothache.' (to Jenny Longuet) It is at this time undoubtedly that Marx composed a vast chronology (90 BC to 1470 AD) in the manner of F C Schlosser's *World History for the German People*.

1882

Preface to the Russian edition of the 'Communist Manifesto'

January-December: Readings of Russian studies (V I Semevsky, A Issayev, G Mineiko, V P Vorontzov). With reference to a letter from Dietzgen: '. . . the unfortunate man has advanced backwards in order to arrive simply at phenomenology. The case seems to me incurable.' (to Engels, January 5) On Eleanor, who has ambitions to become an actress, but does not leave her sick father: 'I would not for the world want the child to think of herself as being sacrificed on the family altar as an old man's nurse.' (to Engels, January 12) The doctors advise Marx to have a holiday in Algiers. With Engels he writes the preface to the Russian edition of the *Communist Manifesto*. (January 20) He leaves London in order to take a cure in Algeria, and stays en route at the Longuets' home in Argenteuil. In Paris he meets Guesde, Deville and Mesa. He stays in Algiers from February 20 to March 2. He suffers from insomnia and lack of appetite. His condition deteriorates as a result of bad weather. 'Between ourselves, you know that few people hate a show of pathos as much as I do; however, it would be untrue to deny that my mind is to a large extent absorbed by the memory of my wife, who was the best part of my life. Tell my daughters in London to write to their old Nick instead of waiting for him to write to them first.' (to Engels, March 1) Marx has frequent meetings with the judge Fermé, a friend of Charles Longuet, who gives him information about the law on landed property among the Arabs and the oppression exercised by the colonial power. 'Among other things, Fermé has recounted what happens in the career of a police court magistrate (which is extremely typical): torture is used to obtain confessions; it is the police who carry it out, of course, as with the English in India, and the judge is supposed to know nothing about it.' (to Engels, April 8) On his doctor's advice, Marx leaves Algiers for Monte Carlo (May 7–June 7). He visits the Casino and describes the spectacle. 'I think that besides Monaco, which would founder without its casino, Nice too – where the aristocratic and adventurous World congregates in the winter months – would not be able to survive as a fashionable resort without the casino of Monte Carlo. And how childish such casinos are when compared with the Stock Exchange!' (to Eleanor, May 28) He visits Argenteuil. Takes the sulphur baths at Enghien. He keeps Engels informed of every detail of his illness, but does not forget politics. Meeting in Paris with Guesde, Lafargue and Deville. Visits to Lausanne and Geneva (August 23–31). Visit to Vevey (end of August–September 18). He hears a (false) report of Bebel's death: 'It is frightful, the greatest misfortune for our party. He had a unique place in the affections of the German (and one could say "European") working class.' (to Engels, September 16) From Paris: 'If the French government – represented by the financial swindler Duclerc – heard I was here . . . it would perhaps send me on a journey without my doctor's permission, since the "Marxists" and the "anti-Marxists", at their respective congresses in Roanne and Saint-Étienne, have done everything to spoil my stay in France. In spite of that I find compensation in the fact that the same Alliance gang – people like Malon, Brousse, etc. – have had their hopes disappointed . . . No one has been taken in by the silent insinuation: Marx is a German, indeed a Prussian; therefore the French Marxists are traitors to their own country; moreover, no one has dared to say it publicly.' (September 30) Marx pays close attention to the Deprez experiments on the long-distance transmission of electricity. He reads L Hospitalier's *Principal Applications of Electricity*. He criticises severely the tactical errors of Lafargue, the 'certificated oracle of scientific socialism', in his struggle against the possibilists. He discovers 'reminiscences on the Bakunin model' penned by Lafargue. Then: 'Longuet as the last Proudhonian and Lafargue as the last Bakuninist! May the Devil take them!' (to Engels, November 11) 'I am not a Marxist.' (Marx's comment, reported by Engels) Marx does not share Bernstein's views on the importance of Malon's and Brousse's organisation. 'The first organisation of real workers' party dates from the Marseille Congress: Malon was then in Switzerland, Brousse was nowhere and the *Prolétaire* – including the unions – was on the defensive.' (to Engels, November 22) Reading on the history of Egypt and the origins of civilisation (J Lubbock). Marx asks Engels to use his influence with the editors of the *Sozialdemokrat* to persuade them to publish documents on the exploitation of the workers in the Prussian State mines, in order to expose the State socialism of Wagener-Bismarck. (December 8) To his daughter Laura: 'Some recent Russian publications, printed in Holy Russia, not abroad, show the great run of my theories in that country. Nowhere is my success more delightful; it gives me that satisfaction that I damage a power, which, besides England, is the true bulwark of the old society.' (December 14) He reads and praises Engels' manuscript on the German mark. (December 18)

1883

January-March: From Ventor, where he has been staying since November 1882, Marx writes to his daughter Eleanor, with reference to the landing of the British troops at Suez and Alexandria. 'In fact, a more shameless hypocritical-Christian conquest than the conquest of Egypt in time of peace. Even Cowen, who is certainly the best of the English parliamentarians, reflects admiringly upon "this heroic deed", "the dazzle of our military parade". Poor Cowen. He is a genuine British "bourgeois" . . . he does not see that the English "grand old man" is only the tool of the other, non-British sly dogs so far as "politics" enters into the event. . .' (January 9) Death of Jenny Longuet. (January 11) Marx's condition worsens; an inflammation of the throat prevents him from speaking and swallowing. A few weeks later a lung abscess develops and Marx dies on March 14. Engels to Bernstein: 'You will have received my telegram. Everything happened very quickly. First the prospects were good; suddenly this morning there was a collapse, and he passed away. In two minutes this brilliant mind ceased to think, at the very moment when the doctors were reasssuring us. What this man has been to us as a theorist and, at decisive moments, in practical affairs, can only be realised by one who passed his whole life close to him. For many years his magisterial view of events will vanish with him from the scene. Such things are far beyond us. The movement continues, but it will miss the man who intervened calmly, opportunely, authoritatively, and who has saved it from going badly astray more than once.' (Engels to Bernstein, March 14) Engels to Sorge the next day: 'all events which have a natural necessity, however terrible they are, bring with them their own consolation. It was so in this case. The doctors' art might perhaps still have assured him years of vegetative existence, the life of a creature without resilience, dragging out his death to the glory of medical technique, instead of ending suddenly. Our Marx could not have borne it. To live, having in front of him so much unfinished work, burning like Tantalus with the desire to complete it, and being unable to do so − for him it would have been a thousand times more .bitter than the kindly death that took him by surprise. 'Death is not a misfortune for him who dies, but for him who survives,' he was wont to say with Epicurus. And to see this powerful, brilliant man vegetate, a human ruin, for the greater glory of medicine, and to be a laughing stock of the philistines whom he had so often crushed when in possession of all his powers − no, it is a thousand times better that we should bear him the day after tomorrow to the same grave where his wife already lies.'

At Marx's graveside, in Highgate Cemetery, Engels delivers a funeral oration celebrating the two 'scientific discoveries' of Marx: 'the law of development of human history' and 'the special law of motion governing the present-day capitalist mode of production' through 'the discovery of surplus-value'. But in Marx the man of science 'was not even half the man'; 'for Marx was before all else a revolutionary. His real mission in life was to contribute, in one way or another, to the overthrow of capitalist society . . ., to the liberation of the modern proletariat, which he was the first to make conscious of its own position and its needs, conscious of the conditions of its emancipation.' (March 17)

Bibliographical Notes

The following works by Maximilien Rubel complement the information given in this *Marx Chronology*:

T B Bottomore and Maximilien Rubel (eds) *Karl Marx: Selected Writings in Sociology and Social Philosophy* London: Watts & Co., 1956

Maximilien Rubel and Margaret Manale *Marx Without Myth* Oxford: Basil Blackwell, 1975. New York: Harper & Row, 1976

Rubel on Marx, with a preface by Joseph O'Malley. New York: Cambridge University Press, 1980

Maximilien Rubel (ed) *Oeuvres de Karl Marx* Paris: Gallimard, 1963. Bibliothèque de la Pléiade

Maximilien Rubel *Karl Marx: Essai de biographie intellectuelle* Paris: 1957

Maximilien Rubel *Bibliographie des oeuvres de Karl Marx* Paris: 1956, 1960

Maximilien Rubel *Marx devant le bonapartisme* Paris-La Haye: 1960

Maximilien Rubel (ed) *Études de marxologie* (20 issues 1959-1978)

Maximilien Rubel *Marx critique du marxisme* Paris: 1974

Maximilien Rubel *Marx/Engels: Die russische Kommune, Kritik eines Mythos* Munich: 1972

Maximilien Rubel *Marx-Chronik* Munich: 3rd ed. 1971

Maximilien Rubel *Stalin in Selbstzeugnissen* Rowohlt 1975

In preparation: Marx Jubilee Edition edited by Maximilien Rubel

Index of Names

Index of Places

Index of Works

Subject Index